SCOTTISH ENDINGS
WRITINGS ON DEATH

SCOTTISH ENDINGS
WRITINGS ON DEATH

COMPILED BY ANDREW MARTIN

INTRODUCTION BY JAMES ROBERTSON

NATIONAL MUSEUMS OF SCOTLAND

Published by the National Museums of Scotland,
Chambers Street, Edinburgh EH1 1JF

© Trustees of the National Museums of Scotland 1996
Introduction © James Robertson 1996

British Library Cataloguing in Publication Data
A catalogue record of this book is available from the British Library
ISBN 0 948636 86 6

Designed by Perilla Kinchin
Printed in Great Britain by Clifford Press Ltd, Coventry

Acknowledgements

The Publisher and Editor wish to thank the following for permission to print
copyright material in this anthology: Carcanet Press Ltd for Hugh MacDiarmid
Crowdieknowe from *Complete Poems*; David Higham Associates for Edith Sitwell *Scotch
Rhapsody* from *Facade*, Duckworth; Valerie Gillies and Scottish Cultural Press for
Valerie Gillies *Viking Boy* from *The Ringing Rock*, Scottish Cultural Press; The
Independent; John Murray (Publishers) Ltd for George Mackay Brown *The Wheel*
from *A Calendar of Love*, Hogarth Press; Random House UK Ltd for Norman MacCaig
So Many Make One from *Collected Poems*; A P Watt Ltd on behalf of Lord Tweedsmuir
for John Buchan *Witchwood* and *The Ballad of Grey Weather* from *The Herd of
Standlan*;

and the following for assistance in tracing material: John Buchan Society; Burns
Federation; the staff of the Local Studies Libraries at Dumfries, Elgin, and Inverness;
W J Hume; Susan Lamb; Tom Martin; Poetry Library, London; Dr Bo Schoene; the
staff of the Scottish Ethnological Archive; Scottish Poetry Library;

and especially our colleagues in the National Museums of Scotland who provided so
many ideas and suggestions, and the NMS Photographic Service.

Every effort has been made to trace the copyright owners of the works included
in this anthology. If any error or oversight has occurred the Publisher would be
grateful for information, and will correct any such errors at the earliest opportunity.

Cover: *Ruins of Holyrood Chapel* Louis Jacques Mande Daguerre 1787-1851.
Courtesy of the Board of Trustees of the National Museums and Galleries on
Merseyside (Walker Art Gallery, Liverpool).
Inside cover: *Funerali di Giacomo III, Re della Gran Brettagna, celebrati per ordine di
Nostro Signore Papa Clemente XIII, l'anno MDCCLXVI.* NMS
Frontispiece: *Gravestones, Glendale, Isle of Skye.* Dave Reed

The Soldier

Oh! if by any unfortunate chance I should happen to die,
In a French field of turnips or radishes I'll lie.
But thinking of it as really Scottish all the time
Because my patriotic body will impart goodness to the slime.
For I've been brought up by the bonnie country of Scotland
Which I like very much indeed with its lochs and its plots of land
And many other picturesque sites which any tourist can see
So long as he is able to pay British Rail the requisite fee.

And you might give a thought too to my decomposing body
As it lies, poor dead thing, under the frog soddy.
For it will be thinking too of my very nice home country
And its weather which is anything but sultry,
And all the exceedingly jocund times I enjoyed there
And frolicked when I was able to in the soggy Scottish air.

J Y Watson

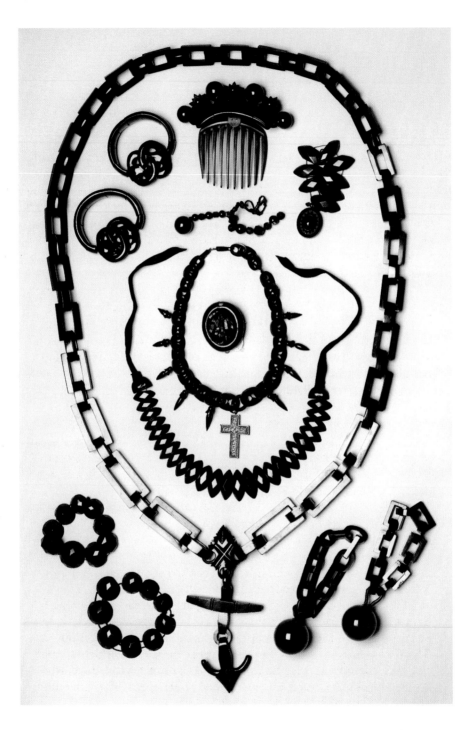

Group of Victorian jet mourning jewellery, worn by Mrs Craig of Edinburgh. NMS

Introduction

Do the Scots have a special relationship with death? It would seem unlikely, and yet the ways of death help to define a culture just as significantly as approaches to living. Alongside the stereotypical images of the parsimonious, canny, calculating Scot, or his wild, extravagant, hell-mend-ye, intoxicated counterpart, there stoops a dour, dry-humoured fatalist, reflecting dismally on what, adapting the Shorter Catechism, might be called 'the chief end of man'. These myths come from somewhere: they may be unhelpful, but they persist.

Unlike many other parts of the world, death has not, at least in recent years, come to Scotland in the form of famine, pestilence, war or natural disaster. When it visits violently through crime or accident, the shock is widely felt and deplored, as one would expect. But it seems that in some respects we have lost a familiarity with death, as a natural conclusion to the process of existence, which is to be regretted. We don't perhaps allow enough death into our lives. This is not meant to be morbid. Two or three generations ago death was very much part of life: people tended to die, as they had been born, in their own homes; but now death is tidied away into hospitals and funeral parlours as if it were a bad-mannered intrusion. This makes it harder for some to cope with bereavement: death is treated as a cruel, unfair negation of life – which, undoubtedly, it sometimes is – instead of an integral part of it.

Partly this has come about because of the decline in religious belief. Dean Ramsay, in his *Reminiscences of Scottish Life and Character* (1858), made the following comments:

> In connection with the awful subject of death and all its concomitants, it has often been remarked that the older generation of Scottish people used to view the circumstances belonging to the decease of their nearest and dearest friends with a coolness which does not at first sight seem consistent with their deep and sincere religious impressions ... There certainly was a quaint and familiar manner in which sacred and solemn subjects were referred to by the older Scottish race, who did not mean to be irreverent, but who no doubt appeared so to a more refined but not really a more religious generation.
>
> It seems to me that this plainness of speech arose in part from the *sincerity* of their belief in all the circumstances of another condition of

being. They spoke of things hereafter as positive certainties, and viewed things invisible through the same medium as they viewed things present.

An event that was seen as little more than a fare-stage, a change of transport on the road to eternity, was bound to lose some of its gravity. Today, by contrast, we are so reluctant to accept the inevitability of death that the search is on for the 'death gene': scientists predict that there is no reason why we may not soon be living to 150. This prospect fills the rest of us, creaking and trauchling through the vale of tears, with horror. My own grandfather, who lived to the age of 96, always reckoned that every year he survived beyond the Biblical span of threescore and ten was a credit to be gratefully acknowledged; but then, he was an accountant, and he knew there was a bottom line. Similar philosophy was once beautifully articulated by an elderly Shetland woman, interviewed in a documentary film, as she spoke of no longer being able to manage the work on her croft: 'Never resent growing old: it's an experience denied to many.' That seems to summarize a thoroughly healthy and positive attitude to the way in which life and death are, naturally, indivisible. It is also an illustration of why discussion of death should not be excluded from daily life; those most at ease and ready to talk about it are often those who live most fully and enthusiastically.

My grandfather enjoyed gentle jokes about death, for example the tendency of funerals to set in train a succession of others, as aged and infirm (and hatless) mourners were quick-chilled by driving wind and rain at the graveside. Graveyard humour, of which there is a large and splendid selection in this book, is a firmly established tradition in Scotland. At the literary end of the spectrum Hugh MacDiarmid's *Crowdieknowe* is a superb poem because it is hard to enjoy its irreverence without at the same time admitting the frisson that its subject matter sends up the spine. Then there is Archibald Geikie's tale of the old couple who were put out at not receiving an invitation to the funeral of one of their friends: 'Never you mind, Tammas,' said the wife, 'we'll be haein' a corp o' our ain before lang, and we'll no ask them.' This is the ridiculous to MacDiarmid's sublime, but there is a common element: at the root of all jokes about death is the notion, how can we dare to make light of something so serious? It can be, of course, that in the darkest moments of grief, to laugh is both a nervous reaction and an intense relief. Since laughter always involves others, it is also confirmation of a shared experience. As Naomi Mitchison once put it, 'In Scottish culture nothing beats a good-going funeral. It takes the mind off other things.'

If it is true that we do not confront death as well as our forebears, this is partly because we are fortunate in not having to deal with it, as they did, in its worst manifestations – carrying off the young and healthy because of appalling social and economic conditions, or because of war, or civil strife and persecution. This book is, in spite of gloomy possibilities, actually remarkably life-affirming: there is certainly as much humour in it as morbidity. We should take our cue from it, and not be so mealy-mouthed about the single, inevitable, incontrovertible fact of all our existences. 'Oor first breath is the beginning o daith' as the proverb has it. Dean Ramsay, again, neatly summed this up in his anecdote about one old Mrs Robison, who

> entertained an inveterate dislike to everything which she thought savoured of *cant*. She had invited a gentleman to dinner on a particular day, and he had accepted with the reservation, 'If I am spared.' – 'Weel, weel,' said Mrs Robison; 'if ye're deid, I'll no expect ye.'

James Robertson

Leith Funeral Establishment, Peat Neuk Close. SEA, NMS

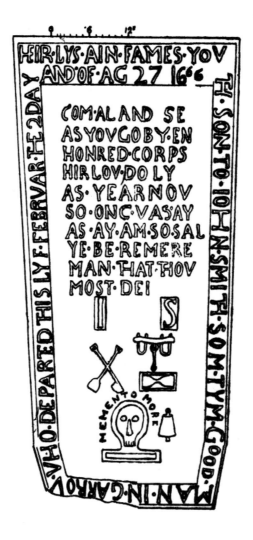

Graveslab at Logie-Pert, Angus, 1666. Proceedings of the Society of Antiquaries
for Scotland 1901–2

Epitaph, Annandale

I Jocky Bell of Braikenbrow, lyes under this stane.
Five of my own sons laid it on my wame;
I liv'd air my dayes, but sturt or strife
Was man o' my meat, and master o' my wife.
If you done better in your time, than I did in mine,
Take this stane aff my wame, and lay it on thine.

Witchcraft and Superstitious Record in the South-western District of Scotland

Mrs Stoba, who lived alone in a cottage at Greenmill, Caerlaverock, died suddenly during the night of Thursday last, from heart failure. Her blind not being drawn up on Friday morning, some neighbours forced the door about half-past ten, and found that she had passed away. It is a singular coincidence that an eight-day clock which had been her property, and is now in the house of her son, the burgh officer of Dumfries, stopped at five minutes before midnight on Thursday, although it was wound up, and there was no apparent reason for the stoppage.

J Maxwell Wood, 1868–1925

A letter to Mr Pepys

John Mackay, of Didril, having put on a new suit of clothes, was told by a Seer that he did see the gallows upon his coat, which he never noticed; but some time after gave his coat to his servant, William Forbes, to whose honesty there could be nothing said at the time, but he was shortly after hanged for theft, with the same coat about him, my informer being an eye-witness of his execution and one who had heard what the Seer said before.

George, Lord Reay, d 1748

Deuterosophia (Second-knowledge)

I was resolved to pay a visit to an English gentleman, Sir William Sacheverill, who had a commission from the English Court of Admirality to give his best tryall to find out gold or money, or any other thing of note, in one of the ships of the Spanish Armada that was blown up in the Bay of Topper-Mory, in the Sound of Mull. And having condescended upon the number of men that were to go with me, one of the number was a handsome boy that waited upon my own person, and, about an hour before I made sail, a woman, that was also one of my own servants, spoke to one of the seamen and bade him dissuade me to take that boy along with me, or, if I did, I should not bring him back alive. The seaman answered he had not confidence to tell me such unwarrantable trifles. I took my voyage and sailed the length of Topper-Mory, and having stayed two or three nights with a Literat and Ingenious Gentleman, who himself had collected many observations of the Second-Sight in the Isle of Man, and compared his notes and mine together, in the end I took leave of him. In the meantime my boy grew sick of a vehement bloody flux, the winds turned so cross that I could neither sail nor row. The boy died with me the eleventh night from his decumbiture, and the seaman to whom the matter was foretold related the whole story when he saw it verifyed. I carried the boy's corpse aboard with me, and after my arrival and his burial I called suddenly for the woman and asked at her what warrand she had to foretell the boy's death. She said that she had no other warrand but that she saw two days before I took my voyage the boy walking with me in the fields, sewed up in his winding sheets from top to toe, and that she had never seen this in others but that she found that they shortly thereafter died, and therefore concluded that he would die too, and that shortly.

Rev John Frazer, 1647–1702

Proverbs

'Oor first breath is the beginning o daith.'

'Daith is deaf, an will hear nae denial.'

The Wheel

After that, Robert walked up the hill between the fields, to a stone house that looked out over the islands and the burning hills. He walked slowly now, as if he was afraid of something.

Even before he reached the door, as he stood lurching and hesitant on the gravel, it was opened by a neat little man with a beard and a grey polo-neck jersey. 'You'll be wanting to know about Walls, ' said the man.

'Yes, captain,' said Robert timidly. 'Maybe you can tell me, for I mind him saying he might be coming to you for a reference, if he decides to go to the whaling next year.'

'I'll tell you,' said the man, 'the same as I've told you every Saturday night for the last two years.'

'No,' said Robert, 'don't tell me that.'

'I will tell you,' said the man, 'for it's the truth, and the sooner you realize it the better.'

'No,' said Robert, 'never mind, I'll go home.'

The old sailor seized him by the arm. 'Listen,' he said, in a loud angry voice. 'Walls is cold and in his grave. Didn't I see him laid out in his coffin when we carried him to the kirkyard? Didn't I put a stone up for him, with his name and his years carved on it?'

Robert shook himself free. He gave the little man one terrified look. Then he turned between the new daffodils and the fuchsia bush on to the road. His feet shuffled and knocked into each other in his haste to be gone.

'You better behave yourself,' yelled the old sailor after him. 'You better not come annoying folk every Saturday night, asking after a dead man! There's places for fools like you! Now I'm warning you!

At home in the little stone house at the edge of the pier, Robert laid the table for two, as he always did, and put on the kettle to boil. He opened a drawer in the dresser and thumbed through a pile of letters and cuttings. At last he found the scrap of newspaper he was looking for. He put on his steel spectacles, and sitting down in the strawback chair beside the fire read the print on it:

'Last Saturday night a sad discovery was made, when the body of a local sailor William Walls was found at low tide among the rocks under his own pier. Mr Walls, who was fifty years of age, was of a jovial disposition, and will be much missed by his many friends in the locality. The news came as a particular shock to Mr Wall's cronies with whom he had spent a happy evening only a matter of hours before the tragic discovery was made. For some years he sailed in the Swallow Line under Captain Stevens, a distinguished son of the islands. Mr Walls was a bachelor, and lived at the South End with his friend Mr Robert Jansen, with whom sympathy is expressed at this time. The funeral, which was well attended, took place to the local cemetery on Tuesday afternoon, and was conducted by Lieutenant Rogers of the Salvation Army, with which sect the deceased had been connected at one period in his career.

Robert carefully replaced the cutting in the drawer. He put a spoon of sugar and a spurt of milk into each cup. He took two eggs out of the box and broke them into the pan; then, after a moment's hesitation, he broke a third egg into the pan.

'Walls is always hungry for his supper on a Saturday night, after the drink,' he murmured. 'What a man for eggs!'

George Mackay Brown, 1921–96

Raw Weather

There's mony a thing we dinna like,
But we maun wi' them just put up;
For, wha the de'il cares what we like,
Or how we feel, or how we sup?

We dinna like the weather raw,
The dawding win', the blashing rain,
Nor sleety showers frae the nor-wast,
And o' the snow we are na fain.

Weel aff are they aneath the mools,
They never fin' the caul ava,
But in their lanely narrow beds
Do snugly doze and rot awa.

The frost may bite, the hail may nip,
The rain may steep us to the skin,
But thae aneath the auld green truffs
The waes o' weather never fin'.

John MacTaggart, 1797–1830

Edinburgh, – January 29. Yesterday died in the Abbey, aged 85, Mr Harry Prentice, who first introduced the culture of potatoes into this country. In 1784 he sunk 140 £ with the Managers of the Canongate Poor House, for a weekly subsistence of 7s. and has since made several small donations to that charity. His coffin, for which he paid two guineas, with 1703, the year of his birth, has hung in his house these nine years; and he has the undertaker's written obligation to screw him down with his own hand gratis. The managers are bound to bury him with a hearse and four coaches, at Restalrig.

Over the grave of a glover of Elgin

> This world is a Cite full of streets,
> And death is the mercat that all men meets,
> If lyfe were a thing that monie could buy,
> The poor could not live and the rich would not die.

Scotch Rhapsody

'Do not take a bath in Jordan,
                    Gordan,
On the holy Sabbath, on the peaceful day!'
Said the huntsman, playing on his old bagpipe,
Boring to death the pheasant and the snipe –
Boring the ptarmigan and grouse for fun –
Boring them worse than a nine-bore gun.
Till the flaxen leaves where the prunes are ripe,
Hear the tartan wind a-droning in the pipe,
And they heard McPherson say:
'Where do the waves go? What hotels
Hide their bustles and their gay ombrelles?
And would there be room? – Would there be *room*?
   Would there be room for me?'
There is a hotel at Ostend
Cold as the wind, without an end,
Haunted by ghostly poor relations
Of Bostonian conversations
(Bagpipes rotting through the walls.)
And there the pearl-ropes fall like shawls
With a noise like marine waterfalls.
And 'Another little drink wouldn't do us any harm'
Pierces through the Sabbatical calm.
And that is the place for me!
So do not take a bath in Jordan, Gordon,
On the holy Sabbath on the peaceful day –
Or you'll never go to heaven, Gordon McPherson,
And speaking purely as a private person
That is the place – *that* is the place – that is the *place* for me!

Dame Edith Sitwell, 1887–1964

Epitaph

Erected to the Memory of John McFarlane
Drown'd in the Water of Leith
By a few affectionate friends.

'The sahib,' he continued, pointing to the grave, 'he not dead. He bury, he not dead.'

My lord uttered a little noise, moved nearer to the grave, and stood and stared in it.

'Buried and not dead?' exclaimed Sir William. 'What kind of rant is this?'

'See, sahib,' said Secundra. 'The sahib and I alone with murderers; try all way to escape, no way good. Then try this way: good way in warm climate, good way in India; Here, in this dam cold place, who can tell? I tell you pretty good hurry you help, you light a fire, help rub.'

'What is the creature talking of?' cried Sir William. 'My head goes round.'

'I tell you I bury him alive,' said Secundra. 'I teach him swallow his tongue. Now dig him up pretty good hurry, and he not much worse. 'You light a fire.'

Sir William turned to the nearest of his men. 'Light a fire,' said he. 'My lot seems to be cast with the insane.'

'You good man,' returned Secundra. 'Now I go dig the sahib up.'

He returned as he spoke to the grave, and resumed his former toil. My lord stood rooted, and I at my lord's side, fearing I knew not what.

The frost was not yet very deep, and presently the Indian threw aside his tool, and began to scoop the dirt by handfuls. Then he disengaged a corner of a buffalo robe; and then I saw hair catch among his finger: yet a moment more, and the moon shone on something white. A while Secundra crouched upon his knees, scraping with delicate fingers, breathing with puffed lips; and when he moved aside I beheld the face of the Master wholly disengaged. It was deadly white, the eyes closed, the ears and nostrils plugged, the cheeks fallen, the nose sharp as if in death; but for all he had lain so many days under the sod, corruption had not approached him, and (what strangely affected all of us) his lips and chin were mantled with a swarthy beard.

'My God!' cried Mountain, 'he was as smooth as a baby when we laid him there!'

'They say hair grows upon the dead,' observed Sir William; but his voice was thick and weak.

Secundra paid no heed to our remarks, digging swift as a terrier in the loose earth. Every moment the form of the Master, swathed in his buffalo robe, grew more distinct in the bottom of that shallow trough; the moon shining strong, and the shadows of the standers-by, as they drew forward and back, falling and flitting over his emergent countenance. The sight held us with a horror not before experienced. I dared not look my lord in the face; but for as long as it lasted, I never observed him to draw breath; and a little in the background one of the men (I know not whom) burst into a kind of sobbing.

'Now,' said Secundra, 'you help me lift him out.'

Of the flight of time, I have no idea; it may have been three hours, and it may have been five, that the Indian laboured to reanimate his master's body. One thing only I know, that it was still night, and the moon was not yet set, although it had sunk low, and now barred the plateau with long shadows, when Secundra uttered a small cry of satisfaction; and, leaning swiftly forth, I thought I could myself perceive a change upon the icy countenance of the unburied. The next moment I beheld his eyelids flutter; the next they rose entirely, and the week-old corpse looked me for a moment in the face.

So much display of life I can myself swear to. I have heard from others that he visibly strove to speak, that his teeth showed in his beard, and that his brow was contorted as with an agony of pain and effort. And this may have been; I know not, I was otherwise engaged. For at that first disclosure of the dead man's eyes, my Lord Durrisdeer fell to the ground, and when I raised him up, he was a corpse.

Day came, and still Secundra could not be persuaded to desist from his unavailing efforts. Sir William, leaving a small party under my command, proceeded on his embassy with the first light; and still the Indian rubbed the limbs and breathed in the mouth of the dead body. You would think such labours might have vitalised a stone; but, except for that one moment (which was my lord's death), the black spirit of the Master held aloof from its discarded clay; and by about the hour of noon, even the faithful servant was at length convinced. He took it with unshaken quietude.

'Too cold,' said he, 'good way in India, no good here.'

Robert Louis Stevenson, 1850–94

Epitaph

Her lys
James Stewart
He sall rys.

St John's Episcopal Church, Edinburgh, seen from the burial ground of
St Cuthbert's. George N Jenkins, SEA, NMS

Last Lauch

The Minister said it wald dee,
the cypress-buss I plantit.
But the buss grew til a tree,
naething dauntit.

It's grawan stark and heich,
derk and strucht and sinister,
Kirkyairdielike and dreich.
But whaur's the Minister?

Douglas Young, 1913–73

Beattock for Moffat

Just at the Summit they stopped an instant to let a goods train pass, and, in a faint voice, the consumptive said, 'I'd almost lay a wager now I'd last to Moffat, Jock. The Shap, ye ken, I aye looked at as the beginning of the run home. The hills, ye ken, are sort o' heartsome. Not that they're bonny hills like Moffat hills, na', na', ill-shapen sort of things, just like Borunty tatties, awfu' puir names, too, Shap Fell and Rowland Edge, Hutton Roof Crags and Arnside Fell; heard ever onybody sich-like names for hills? Naething to fill the mooth; man, the Scotch hills just grap ye in the mooth for a' the world like speerits.' ...

The Eden ran from bank to bank, its water swirling past as wildly as when 'the bauld Buccleugh' and his Moss Troopers, bearing the 'Kinmount' fettered in their midst, plunged in and passed it, whilst the keen Lord Scroope stood on the brink amazed and motionless. Gretna, so close to England, and yet a thousand miles away in speech and feeling, found the sands now flying through the glass. All through the mosses which once were the 'Debateable Land' on which the moss troopers of the clan Graeme were used to hide the cattle stolen from the 'auncient enemy', the now repatriated Scotchman murmured feebly 'that it was bonny scenery' although a drearier prospect of 'moss hags' and stunted birch trees is not to be found. At Ecclefechan he just raised his head, and faintly spoke of 'yon auld carle, Carlyle, ye ken, a dour thrawn body, but a gran' pheelosopher', and then lapsed into silence, broken by frequent struggles to take breath.

His wife and brother sat still, and eyed him as a cow watches a locomotive engine pass, amazed and helpless, and he himself had but the strength to whisper, 'Jock, I'm dune, I'll no see Moffat, blast it, yon smoke, ye ken, yon London smoke has been ower muckle for ma lungs.'

The tearful, helpless wife, not able even to pump up the harmful and unnecessary conventional lie, which, after all, consoles only the liar, sat pale and limp, chewing the fingers of her Berlin gloves. Upon the weather-beaten cheek of Jock glistened a tear, which he brushed off as angrily as if it h'd been a wasp.

'Aye, Andra', he said, 'I would hae liket awfu' weel that ye should win Moffat. Man, the rowan trees are a' in bloom, and there's a bonny breer upon the corn – aye, ou aye, the reid bogs are lookin' gran' the year – but, Andra', I'll tak ye east to the auld kirk-yaird, ye'll no' ken onything aboot it, but we'll hae a heartsome funeral.'

Lockerbie seemed to fly towards them, and the dying Andra' smiled as his brother pointed out the place and said, 'Ye mind, there are no ony Christians in it,' and answered, 'Aye, I mind, naething but Jardines,' as he fought for breath.

The death dews gathered on his forehead as the train shot by Nethercleugh, passed Wamphray and Dinwoodie, and with a jerk pulled up at Beattock just at the summit of the pass.

So in the cold spring morning light, the fine rain beating on the platform, as the wife and brother got their almost speechless care out of the carriage, the brother whispered, 'Dam't, ye've done it, Andra', here's Beattock; I'll tak' ye east to Moffat yet to dee.'

But on the platform, huddled on the bench to which he had been brought, Andra' sat speechless and dying in the rain. The doors banged to, the guard stepped in lightly as the train flew past, and a belated porter shouted, 'Beattock – Beattock for Moffat,' and then, summoning his last strength, Andra' smiled, and whispered faintly in his brother's ear, 'Aye, Beattock – for Moffat!' Then his head fell back, and a faint bloody foam oozed from his pallid lips. His wife stood crying helplessly, the rain beating upon the flowers of her cheap hat, rendering it shapeless and ridiculous. But Jock, drawing out a bottle, took a short dram and saying, 'Andra', man, ye made a richt gude fecht o' it,' snorted an instant in a red pocket-handkerchief, and calling up a boy, said, 'Rin, Jamie, to the toon, and tell McNicol to send up and fetch a corp.' Then, after helping to remove the body to the waiting-room, walked out into the rain, and, whistling 'Corn Rigs' quietly between his teeth, lit up his pipe, and muttered as he smoked, 'A richt gude fecht – man, aye, ou aye, a game yin Andra', puir felly. Weel, weel, he'll hae a braw hurl onyway in the new Moffat hearse.'

R B Cunninghame-Graham, 1852–1936

'In memoriam' card produced for the funeral of Archibald Nichol. NMS

Epitaph, Leslie, Fife

Here lies in the dust Charles Brown
Sometime a wright in London town
Who coming home parents to see
And of his years being twenty-three
Of a decay with a bad host
He died upon the Yorkshire coast.
The 18th of May, 1752
We hope his soul in Heaven rests now.

From *Guy Mannering*

Wasted, weary, wherefore stay,
restling thus with earth and clay?
From the body pass away;–
Hark! the mass is singing.

From these doff thy mortal weed,
Mary Mother be thy speed,
Saints to help thee at thy need;–
Hark! the knell is ringing.

Fear not snow-drift driving fast,
Sleet or hail or levin blast;
Soon the shroud shall lap thee fast,
And the sleep be on thee cast
That shall know no waking.

Haste thee, haste thee, to be gone,
Earth flits fast, and time draws on,–
Gasp thy gasp, and groan thy groan
Day is near the breaking.

Heaven cannot abide it,
Earth refuses to hide it,
Open lock – end strife,
Come death, and pass life.

Sir Walter Scott, 1771–1832

Epitaph, Eyrie, Aberdeenshire

Erected to the memory of Alexander Gray, some time farmer
in Mill of Burns, who died in the 96th year of his age, having
had 32 legitimate children by two wives.

On a Wag in Mauchline

Lament him, Mauchline husbands a',
He often did assist ye;
For had ye staid whole weeks awa',
Your wives they ne'er had missed ye.

Ye Mauchline bairns, as on ye pass,
To school in bands thegither,
Oh, tread ye lightly on his grass,
Perhaps he was your father.

Robert Burns, 1759–96

Old tomb in Warrender Park, Edinburgh. Old and New Edinburgh, by
James Grant, NMS

That morning Mrs Carlyle wrote her daily letter to Carlyle, and took it herself to the post. In the afternoon she went out in her brougham for the usual drive round Hyde Park, taking her little dog with her. Nero lay under a stone in the garden in Cheyne Row, but she loved all kinds of animals, dogs especially, and had found another to succeed him. Near Victoria Gate she had put the dog out to run. A passing carriage went over its foot, and, more frightened than hurt, it lay on the road on its back crying. She sprang out, caught the dog in her arms, took it with her into the brougham, and was never more seen alive. The coachman went twice round the drive, by Marble Arch down to Stanhope Gate, along the Serpentine and round again. Coming a second time near to the Achilles statue, and surprised to receive no directions, he turned round, saw indistinctly that something was wrong, and asked a gentleman near to look into the carriage. The gentleman told him briefly to take the lady to St. George's Hospital, which was not two hundred yards distant. She was sitting with her hands folded on her lap dead.

I had stayed at home that day, busy with something, before going out in the evening. A servant came to the door, sent by the housekeeper at Cheyne Row, to say that something had happened to Mrs Carlyle, and to beg me to go at once to St George's. Instinct told me what it must be. I went to Geraldine; she was getting ready for the party, and supposed that I had called to take her there. I told her the message which I had received. She flung a cloak about her, and we drove to the hospital together. There, on a bed in a small room, we found Mrs Carlyle, beautifully dressed, dressed as she always was, in quietly perfect taste. Nothing had been touched. Her bonnet had not been taken off. It was as if she had sate upon the bed after leaving the brougham, and had fallen back upon it asleep. But there was an expression on the face which was not sleep, and which, long as I had known her, resembled nothing which I had ever seen there. The forehead, which had been contracted in life by continued pain, had spread out to its natural breadth, and I saw for the first time how magnificent it was. The brilliant mockery, the sad softness with which the mockery alternated, both were alike gone. The features lay composed in a stern majestic calm. I have seen many beautiful faces in death, but never any so grand as hers. I can write no more of it.

James Anthony Froude, 1818–94

Proverbs

'Am fear fhaide bha beò riamh, fhuair e 'm bàs.'
('The oldest man that ever lived, died at last.')

'Amaisidh an dall air an reilig.'
('A blind man will find his way to the burial ground.')

*Black oval brooch with 'gold' framework and backing, with a central oval
arrangement of hair, and a length of black cord. NMS*

So Many Make One

There are so many deaths that go
To make up death, as a grown man
Is the walking grave of boy after boy.
– Sometimes we see in him the frown
Of a forsaken ghost, or a dead boy
Speaks suddenly in a petulant voice;
Six feet of blood have drowned so many.
And when death itself comes face to face

With us round that dreadful turning, will
All its ancestors be alive –
Will we, one moment, in its smile
See innocence and belief and love?

Norman MacCaig, 1910–96

The Buchanites, from *The Scottish Gallovidian Encyclopedia*

A singular sect of religious fanatics that first made their appearance in
the neighbourhood of Glasgow. Their founder was a Mrs Buchan, the wife
of a dyer in Glasgow. One of her chief tenets was, that all who followed
her and her doctrine would go to heaven without tasting of death,
like Elias, and that too, on a certain day which she prophesied – for she
always wished to be looked on as a prophetess, and that she alighted on
earth at the *Clauchan o' Thornhill*, from heaven, keeping still the *litt vats* in
the gorbals of Glasgow out of sight. At long and length the glorious day

arrived on which they were all to be taken to the regions above, where endless happiness existed, and pleasure for evermore. Platforms were erected for them to wait on, until the wonderful hour arrived, and Mrs Buchan's platform was exalted above all the others. The hair of *ilka* head was cut short – all but a tuft on the top, for the angels to catch by when drawing them up. The momentous hour came. Every station for ascension was instantly occupied. Thus they stood, expecting to be wafted every moment into the land of bliss, when a gust of wind came; – but, instead of wafting them upwards, it capsized Mrs Buchan, platform and all! and the fall made her all *hech* again on the *cauld yird*. After this unexpected downcome, she fell into disgrace by her leaders, and her words had not so much weight with them; still, however, a great number clung by her; and one night (she having been ailing for some time before) a fit came on her, out of which she never recovered; but her disciples, thinking it to be a trance into which she had fallen, expected her to awake; but no signs of this appearing for some days, and her body beginning to have a putrid smell, they thought it prudent to bury it in the earth beside the house; and by her have been laid all those of her sect who have since died.

John MacTaggart 1797–1830

Epitaph, Hutton

In memory of
Donald Campbell, Esq of Barbreek, N B

He died June 5th, 1801, aged 53 years. With
talents and a heart that might have rendered
him useful in Society in his career through life,
he unfortunately ran to the wrong side of the post,
and owing to peculiar circumstances, has experienced a good deal of worldly persecution, but
looks up to a merciful God (who always knows
our most inmost motives) for everlasting bliss.

Epitaph from Aberdeen

Here lie the bones of Elizabeth Charlotte
Born a virgin, died a harlot
She was aye a virgin at seventeen
A remarkable thing in Aberdeen.

My Hoggie

What will I do gin my hoggie die?
My joy, my pride, my hoggie!
My only beast, I had nae mae,
And vow but I was vogie!

The lee-lang night we watch'd the fauld,
Me and my faithfu' doggie;
We heard nought but the roaring linn,
Amang the braes sae scroggie;

But the houlet cry'd frae the castle wa',
The blitter frae the boggie,
The tod reply'd upon the hill,
I trembl'd for my hoggie.

When day did daw, and cocks did craw,
The morning it was foggie;
An unco tyke lap o'er the dyke,
And maist has kill'd my hoggie.

Robert Burns, 1759–96

The Auld Man's Mear's Dead

The auld man's mear's dead;
The auld man's mear's dead;
The auld man's mear's dead,
A mile aboon Dundee.

There was hay to ca', and lint to lead,
A hunner hotts o' muck to spread,
And peats and truffs and a' to lead –
And yet the jaud to dee!

The auld man's mear's dead;
The auld man's mear's dead;
The auld man's mear's dead,
A mile aboon Dundee.

She had the fiercie and the fleuk,
The wheezloch and the wanton yeuk;
On ilka knee she had a breuk –
What ail'd the beast to dee?

The auld man's mear's dead;
The auld man's mear's dead;
The auld man's mear's dead,
A mile aboon Dundee.

He's thinkin' on the by-gane days,
And a' her douce and canny ways;
And houw his ain gude-wife, auld Bess,
Micht maist as weel been spared.

Patrick Birnie, b 1635

The Independent 16 August 1995

News of a sad freak accident, also in Scotland. At the Lairg Crofter's Show in Sutherland last Saturday, a terrier, Beenie, got in the way of a caber. Eileen MacKay, secretary of the show and the dog's co-owner, said: 'The competitor tossed the caber and unfortunately it did not go the right way. Everyone scattered immediately. Beenie had been running about. We called her but she never heard and it landed right on top of her.' The local vet was called but, sadly, Beenie had broken her neck. 'It was a tragic end to a great day,' said Mrs MacKay.

Pet cemetery, Newcraighall. Mark Collard

The Starlaw Disaster

It was 18 and 70, Aprile the ninth day;
Ninety-six men and boys for their work took their way.
In health and in strength down the shaft they did go,
Never dreaming of how many would lie low.

For about twelve o'clock on that same fatal day,
'The pit-shaft's on fire!', the roadsman did say.
And quick through the workins the alarum he gave,
All praying to their maker their sweet lives to save.

All eagerly ran to get on to the cage,
But the fire in the shaft like a furnace did rage.
All praise to young John Steel who at the engine did stand,
And forty-eight safe on the bank he did land.

William Ralston, William Rushford and young David Muir,
By that terrible disaster you will see them no more.
Patrick and Peter M'Comiskie, aye, and Swanson likewise,
By that terrible disaster in their cold grave now lies.

Now widows and orphans who are now left to murn,
By that awful disaster they will never return.
But God is so merciful, as all mankind knows,
He will share in their sorrow, and soften their woes.

Traditional

Epitaph, Cross Kirk, Normavine, Shetland

Donald Robertson.
Born 1st of January, 1785, died 4th of June, 1848
Aged 63 years

He was a peaceable quiet man, and to all appearance a
sincere Christian. His death was very much regretted,
which was caused by the stupidity of Laurence Tulloch,
of Clotherton, who sold him nitre instead of Epsom salts,
by which he was killed in the space of 3 hours after taking
a dose of it.

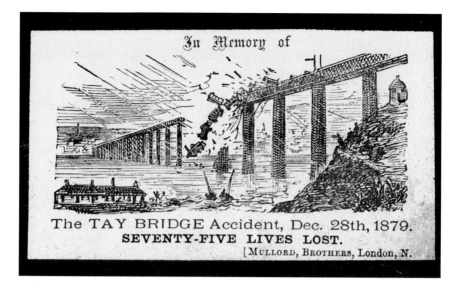

'In memoriam' card produced after the Tay Bridge collapse. NMS

Scenes and Legends of the North of Scotland

In a central part of the churchyard of Nigg there is a rude, undressed stone, near which the sexton never ventures to open a grave. A wild apocryphal tradition connects the erection of this stone with the times of the quarantine fleet. The plague, as the story goes, was brought to the place by one of the vessels, and was slowly flying along the ground, disengaged from every vehicle of infection, in the shape of a little yellow cloud. The whole country was alarmed, and groups of people were to be seen on every eminence, watching with anxious horror the progress of the little cloud. They were relieved, however, from their fears and the plague by an ingenious man of Nigg, who, having provided himself with an immense bag of linen, fashioned somewhat in the manner of a fowler's net, cautiously approached the yellow cloud, and, with a skill which could have owed nothing to previous practice, succeeded in enclosing the whole of it in the bag. He then secured it by wrapping it up carefully, fold after fold, and fastening it down with pin after pin; and as the linen was gradually changing, as if under the hands of the dyer, from white to yellow, he consigned it to the churchyard, where it has slept ever since.

Hugh Miller, 1802–56

The first death from cholera in Dumfries occurred on the 15th of September. For the 1st of October the record showed fifty-six new cases and twenty-three deaths, while the next day it reached its culminating point, rising to fifty-five new cases and fifty-four deaths. Fatal cases continued to occur daily till the 30th October, which proved a blank day; and by the middle of November the disease had fairly disappeared. During its stay it desolated scores of homesteads, leaving 'many a sweet babe fatherless, and many a widow mourning,' and sometimes sweeping whole families into eternity. As officially reported, 837 persons were attacked, of whom 421 died; but the number of coffins made, and the heavy sexton's bills, as based upon the burial-roll, went to shew that the real deaths were greater in number and probably not fewer than 550. The sister burgh of Maxwelltown suffered about as much, population considered, the cases there having been 237, and the deaths 127. Beneath the turf, on which we now gaze – kept green even in winter by the rich soil below – at least 350 coffined bodies were laid, piled tier upon tier, with quicklime scattered between. The cavity was made eighteen feet deep, and extended as the demand for accommodation rapidly and fearfully increased, and the grave-diggers had to ply their implements in harmony, with the dismal Deathstave; 'I gather them in; I gather them in!'

William McDowall, 1815–88

Greyfriars Churchyard, Edinburgh. John Elphinstone, NMS

Witch Wood

Peter Pennecuik, sitting on the stone by the smithy door and mopping a wet forehead, watched Amos drop his tools heavily as he returned from a job at Reiverslaw.

'What mak' ye o' the weather?' he asked.

Amos straightened his back.

'I dinna like it. The gillyflowers in my yaird are ettlin' to bloom. My grannie had a verse o' auld Thomas the Rhymer – what was it? – :

A Yule wi'out snaws

A Januar' wi' haws

Bring the deid thraws.

'There's a judgment preparin', ' said Peter, 'but whatna kind o' judgment I daurna guess. Certes, it's no canny.'

'I've heard o' nane ailin', but there's seeckness comin'. I can smell it in the air, and the brute beasts can smell it, for they've sweir to come near Woodilee. There's no a tod or a maukin on a' the Hill o' Deer. D'ye no find

33

a queer savour in the countryside, Peter? There's wind enough to shake the saughs, but the warld smells like the inside o' a press-bed when the door's steekit. Oh for a snell, dirlin' blast! There's something rotten and stawsome and unearthly about the blue lift and the saft air. It's like withered floo'ers on a midden. ... If there's nae seeckness yet, there's seeckness on the road. I maun awa in and see to Ailie, for this morn she was complaining o' a sair heid.'

Two days later the child of a cotter at Mirehope returned from school in the manse kitchen and to his mother's amazement beat his head against the door. He fell asleep on the wedder's skin beside the fire, and when he was awakened for his supper his cheeks were flaming and he seemed to have difficulty with his speech. He was put with the rest into the box which was the children's bed, and all night filled it with his cries, so that the others sought peace on the floor. In the morning his face and throat were swollen, his eyes were sightless, and he struggled terribly for breath. Before noon he was dead.

In this way came the plague to Woodilee.

John Buchan, 1875–1940

Storms

The accounts were most dismal; the country was a charnel-house. The first day he brought us tidings of the loss of thousands of sheep, and likewise of the death of Robert Armstrong a neighbour shepherd, one whom we all well knew, he having but lately left the Blackhouse to herd on another farm. He died not above 300 paces from a farm house while at the same time it was known to them all that he was there. His companion left him at a dike side, and went in to procure assistance; yet, nigh as it was, they could not reach him, though they attempted it again and again; and at length they were obliged to return, and suffer him to perish at the side of the dike. There were three of my own intimate acquaintances perished that night. There was another shepherd named Watt, the circumstances of whose death were peculiarly affecting. He had been to see his sweetheart on the night before with whom he had finally agreed and settled every thing about the marriage; but it so happened in the inscrutable awards of providence, that at the very time when the banns of his marriage were proclaimed in the church of Moffat, his companions were carrying him home a corpse from the hill.

It may not be amiss here to remark that it was a received opinion all over the country, that sundry lives were lost, and a great many more endangered by the administering of ardent spirits to the sufferers while in a state of exhaustion. It was a position against which I entered my vehement protest, nevertheless the voice of the multitude should never be disregarded. A little bread and sweet milk, or even a little bread and cold water, it was said, proved a much safer restorative in the fields. There is no denying that there were some who took a glass of spirits that night, that never spoke another word, even though they were continuing to walk when their friends found them. On the other hand, there was one woman who left the children, and followed her husband's dog, who brought her to his master lying in a state of insensibility. He had fallen down bare-headed among the snow, and was all covered over save one corner of his plaid. She had nothing better to take with her when she set out than a bottle of sweet milk and a little oatmeal cake, and yet with the help of these she so far recruited his spirits as to get him safe home, though not without long and active perseverence. She took two little vials with her, and in these she heated the milk in her bosom. That man would not be disposed to laugh at the silliness of the fair sex for some time.

It is perfectly unaccountable how easily people died that night. The frost must certainly have been prodigious; so intense as to have seized on the vitals of those that overheated themselves by wading and toiling too impatiently among the snow, a thing that is very aptly done. I have conversed with five or six that were carried home in a state of insensibility that night who never would again have moved from the spot where they lay, and were only brought to life by rubbing and warm applications, and they uniformly declared that they felt no kind of pain or debility, farther than an irresistible desire to sleep. Many fell down while walking, and speaking, in a sleep so sound as to resemble torpidity, and there is little doubt that those who perished slept away in the same manner. I knew a man well whose name was Andrew Murray, that perished in the snow on Minchmoor, and he had taken it so deliberately that he had buttoned his coat, and folded his plaid, which he had laid beneath his head for a bolster.

James Hogg, 1770–1835

Proverb

'Daith comes in an speirs nae questions.'

Dog mourning its little master, A Archer. City of Edinburgh Art Centre

Margaret Ogilvy

She had a son who was far away at school. I remember very little about him, only that he was a merry-faced boy who ran like a squirrel up a tree and shook the cherries into my lap. When he was thirteen and I was half his age the terrible news came, and I have been told the face of my mother was awful in its calmness as she set off to get between Death and her boy. We trooped with her down the brae to the wooden station, and I think I was envying her the journey in the mysterious wagons; I know we played around her, proud of our right to be there, but I do not recall it, I only speak from hearsay. Her ticket was taken, she had bidden us good-bye with that fighting face which I cannot see, and then my father came out of the telegraph-office and said huskily, 'He's gone!' Then we turned very quietly and went home again up the little brae. But I speak from hearsay no longer; I knew my mother for ever now.

That is how she got her soft face and her pathetic ways and her large charity, and why other mothers ran to her when they had lost a child. 'Dinna greet, poor Janet,' she would say to them; and they would answer, 'Ah, Margaret, but you're greeting yoursel.' Margaret Ogilvy had been her maiden name, and after the Scotch custom she was still Margaret Ogilvy to her old friends. Margaret Ogilvy I loved to name her. Often when I was a boy, 'Margaret Ogilvy, are you there?' I would call up the stair.

She was always delicate from that hour, and for many months she was very ill. I have heard that the first thing she expressed a wish to see was the christening robe, and she looked long at it and then turned her face to the wall. That was what made me as a boy think of it always as the robe in which he was christened, but I knew later that we had all been christened in it, from the oldest of the family to the youngest, between whom stood twenty years.

My mother lay in bed with the christening robe beside her, and I peeped in many times at the door and then went to the stair and sat on it and sobbed. I know not if it was that first day, or many days afterwards, that there came to me my sister, the daughter my mother loved the best; yes, more I am sure even than she loved me, whose great glory she has been since I was six years old. This sister, who was then passing out of her 'teens, came to me with a very anxious face and wringing her hands, and she told me to go ben to my mother and say to her that she still had another boy. I went ben excitedly, but the room was dark, and when I heard the door shut and no sound come from the bed I was afraid, and stood still. I suppose I was breathing hard, or perhaps I was crying, for a after a time I heard a listless voice that had never been listless before say, 'Is that you?' I think the tone hurt me, for I made no answer, and then the voice said more anxiously 'Is that you?' again. I thought it was the dead boy she was speaking to, and I said in a little lonely voice, 'No, it's no' him, it's just me.' Then I heard a cry, and my mother turned in bed, and though it was dark I knew that she was holding out her arms.

J M Barrie, 1860–1937

Proverb

'Daith comes in an it's no particular who it taks awa.'

The Tragic Death of the Rev A H Mackonochie

Friends of humanity, of high and low degree,
I pray ye all come listen to me;
And truly I will relate to ye,
The tragic fate of the Rev Alexander Heriot Mackonochie.

Who was on a visit to the Bishop of Argyle,
For the good of his health, for a short while;
Because for the last three years his memory had been affected,
Which prevented him from getting his thoughts collected.

'Twas on Thursday, the 15th of December, in the year 1887,
He left the Bishop's house to go and see Loch Leven;
And he was accompanied by a little Skye terrier and a deer-hound,
Besides the Bishop's two dogs, that knew well the ground.

And as he had taken the same walk the day before,
The Bishop's mind was undisturbed and easy on that score;
Besides the Bishop had been told by some men,
That they saw him making his way up a glen.

From which a river flows down with a mighty roar,
From the great mountains of the Mamore;
And this route led him towards trackless wastes eastward,
And no doubt to save his life he had struggled very hard.

And as Mr Mackonochie had not returned at dinner time,
The Bishop ordered two men to search for him, which they didn't
    decline;
Then they searched for him along the road he should have returned,
But when they found him not, they sadly mourned.

And when the Bishop heard it, he procured a carriage and pair,
While his heart was full of woe, and in a state of despair;
He organised three search parties without delay,
And headed one of the parties in person without dismay.

And each party searched in a different way,
But to their regret at the end of the day;
Most unfortunately no discovery had been made,
Then they lost hope of finding him, and began to be afraid.

And as a last hope, two night searches were planned,
And each party with well lighted lamps in hand
Started on their perilous mission, Mr Mackonochie to try and find,
In the midst of driving hail, and the howling wind.

One party searched a distant sporting lodge with right good will,
Besides through brier, and bush, and snow, on the hill;
And the Bishop's party explored the Devil's Staircase with hearts full
    of woe,
A steep pass between the Kinloch hills and the hills of Glencoe.

Oh! it was a pitch dark and tempestuous night,
And the searchers would have lost their way without lamp light;
But the brave searchers stumbled along for hours, but slow,
Over rocks, and ice, and sometimes through deep snow.

And as the Bishop's party were searching they met a third party from
    Glencoe side,
Who had searched bracken and burn, and the country wide;
And sorrow was depicted in each one's face,
Because of the Rev Mr Mackonochie they could get no trace.

But on Saturday morning the Bishop set off again,
Hoping that the last search wouldn't prove in vain;
Accompanied with a crowd of men and dogs,
All resolved to search the forest and the bogs.

And the party searched with might and main,
Until they began to think their search would prove in vain;
When the Bishop's faithful dogs raised a pitiful cry,
Which was heard by the searchers near by.

Then the party pressed on right manfully,
And sure enough there were the dogs guarding the body of
    Mackonochie;
And the corpse was cold and stiff, having been long dead,
Alas! almost frozen, and a wreath of snow around the head.

And as the searchers gathered round the body in pity they did stare,
Because his right foot was stained with blood, and bare;
But when the Bishop o'er the corpse had offered up a prayer,
He ordered his party to carry the corpse to his house on a bier.

So a bier of sticks was most willingly and quickly made,
Then the body was tenderly upon it laid;
And they bore the corpse and laid inside the Bishop's private chapel,
Then the party took one sorrowful look and bade the corpse farewell.

William McGonagall, 1825–1902

Red leather case containing hair arranged for inclusion in articles of jewellery. NMS

Observations on a Tour Through the Highlands

Her body was embowelled and embalmed, and soon afterwards sent over
to Scotland. It was landed, and lay at Leith for some time in a cellar, and
was afterwards carried to Kilsyth, and buried in great pomp, according to
the form of the church of England. It is not twenty years since some of
the inhabitants of this parish died, who were in their youth eye-witnesses
of the funeral.

The body was inclosed, first in a coffin of fir, next in a leaden coffin, nicely cemented, but without any inscription; this was again covered with a very strong wooden coffin. The space between the two was filled up with a white matter, somewhat of the colour and consistence of putty, apparently composed of gums and perfumes, for it had a rich and delicious flavour. When I was a boy at school, I have frequently seen the coffin in which she lies, for the vault was then always accessible, and often opened: but at that time the wooden coffin was entire. Indeed it was only within a few years that it decayed. Even after this, the lead one remained entire for a considerable time; but being very brittle and thin, it also began to moulder away; a slight touch of the finger penetrated any part of it. In the apertures thus made, nothing was seen but the gummy matter above mentioned. When this was partly removed, which was easily done, being very soft, and only about an inch in thickness, another wooden coffin appeared, which seemed quite clear and fresh.

The mummy of Lady Kilsyth. NMS

But no one ever thought of opening it, till the spring 1796, when some rude regardless young men went to visit the tomb, and with sacrilegious hands tore open the leaden coffin. To their surprise, they found under the lead a covering of fir, as clean and fresh as if it had been made the day before. The cover of this being loose, was easily removed. With astonishment and consternation, they saw the body of Lady Kilsyth, and her child, as perfect as the hour they were entombed.

For some weeks this circumstance was kept secret, but at last it began to be whispered in several companies, and soon excited great and general curiosity. On the 12th of June, while I was from home, great crowds assembled, and would not be denied admission. At all hours of the night as well as the day, they afterwards persisted in gratifying their curiosity.

I saw the body soon after the coffin was opened. It was quite entire. Every feature, and every limb was as full, nay the very shroud was as clear and fresh, and the colours of the ribbons as bright as the day they were lodged in the tomb.

What rendered this scene more striking, and truly interesting, was, that the body of her son and only child, the natural heir of the title and estates of Kilsyth, lay at her knee. His colour was as fresh, and his flesh as plump and full, as in the perfect glow of health; the smile of infancy and innocence sat on his lips. His shroud was not only entire, but perfectly clean, without a particle of dust upon it. He seems to have been only a few months old.

The body of Lady Kilsyth was equally well preserved, and at a little distance, with the feeble light of a taper, it would not have been easy to distinguish whether she was dead or alive. The features, nay the very expression of her countenance, were marked and distinct, and it was only in a certain light that you could distinguish any thing like the ghastly and agonizing traits of a violent death. Not a single fold of her shroud was discomposed, nor a single member impaired.

Thomas Garnett, 1766–1802, quoting Rev Robert Rennie

The Scotsman 16 July 1836

About three weeks ago, while a number of boys were amusing themselves in searching for rabbit burrows on the north-east range of Arthur's Seat, they noticed, in a very rugged and secluded spot, a small opening in one of the rocks, the peculiar appearance of which attracted their attention. The mouth of this little cave was closed by three thin pieces of slatestone, rudely cut at the upper ends into a conical form, and so placed as to protect the interior from the effects of the weather. The boys having removed these tiny slabs, discovered an aperture about twelve inches square, in which were lodged seventeen Lilliputian coffins, forming two tiers of eight each, and one on a third just begun!

Each of the coffins contained a miniature figure of the human form cut out in wood, the faces in particular being pretty well executed. They were dressed from head to foot in cotton clothes, and decently 'laid out' with mimic representation of all the funereal trappings which usually form the last habiliments of the dead. The coffins are about three or four inches in length, regularly shaped, and cut out from a single piece of wood, with the exception of the lids, which are nailed down with wire sprigs or common brass pins. The lid and sides of each are profusely studded with ornaments formed of small pieces of tin, and inserted in the wood with great care and regularity. Another remarkable circumstance is, that many years must have elapsed since the first interment took place in this mysterious sepulchre; and it is also evident that the depositions must have been made singly, and at considerable intervals – facts in indicated by the rotten and decayed state of the first tier of coffins and their wooden mummies – the wrapping clothes being in some instances entirely moulded away, while others show various degrees of decomposition; and the coffin last places, with its shrouded tenant, are as clean and fresh as if only a few days had elapsed since their entombment.

As before stated, there were in all seventeen of these mystic coffins; but a number were destroyed by the boys pelting them at each other as unmeaning and contemptible trifles.

Miniature coffins with lids and carved figures, found in a niche on Arthur's Seat, Edinburgh, in 1836. NMS

Viking Boy

a sandstorm strips the dune
to bare-bones
on a straw mat
over a bed of feathers
the boy lies
a hoop of metal
shelters his head
the shield over his face
the sword by his flank
he has a bone comb
not a yellow hair in it
the bed to soften
the blow to the boy
the shield to hide
his young face
from the sharp scatter
from the first handful of sand

Valerie Gillies, b 1948

Collared burial urn from Banffshire, around 1700 BC. NMS

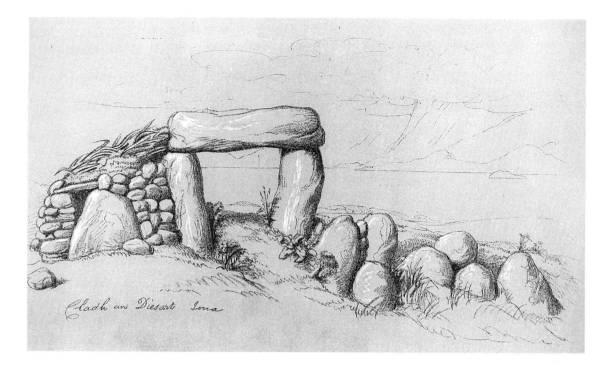

The Cladh an Diseart, 'burial place in the desert', near the cathedral at Iona, was one of the supposed burial places of St Columba. The upper stone of the trilithon was removed in case it should fall and injure cattle. Sculptured Monuments in Iona and the Highlands, by James Drummond, NMS

Memoirs of the Anthropological Society of London, 1866
Bressay, Shetland

And here it may be interesting to give a few instances of the preservation of the human body in peat, for it becomes of the greatest importance to understand that varieties of peat may so entirely differ in their chemical components, as to have entirely opposite effect. I examined the whole locality for coffins, and the last that could be found was opened in the presence of several friends from Lerwick; it turned out to be the most interesting we had yet discovered. Situated rather lower in the peat than the remainder, when we came on it the top appeared more solid, and we soon found it was filled with water, and we proceeded to make a drain and let the water out from the bottom, so as to be able carefully to examine the contents of the coffin. Before letting out the water we observed, on taking up the lid, that a body apparently pretty perfect remained for us. I preserved a portion of the water for chemical analysis. In cleaning the skull and the long bones I found considerable difficulty, and also in separating the skin and muscles of the arm from the bone. I had an easy task in scalping the long sought for treasure, and found that with one grip I had a pretty good wig in my hand. When the men who dug up this coffin saw the contents, they could not be got to render any further assistance, and declared the sight and smell had turned their 'inside out', this was, however, purely the effect of imagination. It was with some difficulty I could get them to bring some clean water to me, and to deposit it at some yards distant. I had gone to Lerwick for a packing case, and the sailors who brought me over hesitated to take back a skeleton, but an offer of a little extra coin of the realm, quite satisfied their consciences.

James Hunt, 1833–69

Crowdieknowe

Oh to be at Crowdieknowe,
When the last trump blaws,
An' see the deid come loupin' owre
The auld grey wa's.

Muckle men wi' tousled beards,
I grat at as a bairn,
'll scramble frae the croodit clay
Wi' feck o' swearin'.

An' glower at God an' a' his gang
O' angels i' the lift,
Thae trashy bleezin' French-like folk
Wha gar'd them shift!

Fain the weemun-folk'll seek
To mak' them haud their row,
Fegs, God's no blate gin he stirs up
The men o' Crowdieknowe!

Hugh MacDiarmid, 1892–1978

Scottish Reminiscences

A curious attitude of mind towards one who has died, but is still unburied, is shown by the use of the word 'corp', which is popularly supposed to be the singular of 'corpse'. This usage may be illustrated by an incident told me by the late Henry Drummond as having occurred in his own experience. While attending the funeral of a man with whom he had had no acquaintance, he enquired of one of the company what employment the deceased had followed. The person questioned did not know, but at once asked his next neighbour, 'I'm sayin', Tam, what was the corp to trade?'

An old couple were exceedingly annoyed that they had not been invited to the funeral of one of their friends. At last the good wife consoled her husband thus: 'Aweel, never you mind, Tammas, maybe we'll be haein' a corp o' our ain before lang, and we'll no ask them.'

A gentleman came to a railway station where he found a mourning party. Wishing to be sympathetic, he enquired of one of the company whether it was a funeral, and received the reply: 'We canna exactly ca' it a funeral, for the corp has missed the railway connection.'

Archibald Geikie, 1835–1924

Epitaph, Prestonpans

William Mathieson here lies,
Whose age was forty-one;
February 17 he dies,
Went Isbel Mitchell from,
Who was his married wife,
The fourth part of his life.
The soul it cannot die
Though the body be turned to clay.
Yet meet again they must,
At the last day
Trumpets shall sound, archangels cry,
Come forth Isbel Mitchell
And meet Will Mathieson in the sky!

Epitaph, Wigtown, Galloway

Here lies
JOHN TAGGART
of honest fame
of stature low
&
a leg lame.
Content was he
with portion small
kept a shop in Wigtown
&
that's all.

Accounts of the Funeral of James VI

Abraham Greene. For vessells of lead for Entombeinge of his Royall Corps and bowells.

Abraham Greene for Entombing of the Royall corps of our late soveraigne King James with lead sodder and workemanship being done at Theobalds. Item more for one vessell of lead to putt in the bowells of his Ryall Majestie with sodder and workemanship £XXV

Paid to Maximilian Coult for makeing the body for the representacion with severall joynts in the armes leggs and body to be moved to severall postures and for setting uyp the same in Westminster Abbey and for his attendances there £X

Item for a crowne of wood and a Lyon upon it for his majesties creast xls

Item for painting the face and hands of the last representation xls

Item for the makeing of a better crowne the former being broaken by the often removeing of the representation and for the guilding of the same being sett with divers stones £X

Daniel Parkes For two Periwiggs

Paid to Daniel Parkes for makeing of one periwigg beard and eyebrows for the body at Denmark house £X

Opposite: *A plate from Funerali di Giacomo III, Re della Gran Brettagna, 1766. James Francis Edward Stuart, father of Bonnie Prince Charlie and known to his enemies as the Old Pretender, was never crowned as James III. NMS*

48

Memorials of St Michael's

In memory of
ROBERT BURNS
who died the 21st July 1796,
in the 37th year of his age.

The foundation-stone of the Mausoleum was laid on the 5th of June 1815, and the building was completed in the following September, the entire cost amounting to about £1500.

When the tomb was finished, it was still an imposing casket without its congenial gem, or like a gorgeous throne without an occupant. The solemn duty of conveying the dust of Burns from the north-east corner to the new home provided for it by the nation was devolved upon four gentlemen – Mr William Grierson, the secretary to the committee; Mr James Thomson, superintendent of the monument; Mr Milligan, builder; and Mr James Bogie, gardener, Terraughty. We have never seen any adequate reason assigned for having this delicate, yet highly honourable, process of exhumation and reinterment done privily and as it were by stealth. However, a secret, quiet mode of procedure, which had some slight advantages of its own, was resolved upon; and accordingly the above named gentlemen, an hour or two before 'the witching time' of midnight, on the 19th of September 1815, hied to the spot pointed out in a previous chapter, and, aided by a small body of workmen, laid bare the earthen bed in which the poet, after 'life's fitful fever,' had 'slept well' since 1796. Beside him lay the remains of his two young sons, Maxwell Burns and Francis Wallace Burns. The coffins of the boys were nearly entire, and, after being placed in shells, were carried to the Mausoleum vault; but in the case of the bard 'the chest that had neither key nor lock' had been already tampered with by the rifling fingers of decay. At first sight the venerated contents seemed marvellously perfect, suggesting the idea of one who had just sunk into the slumber of death, the lordly forehead of the dreamless sleeper still rising arched and high, the 'dome of thought' covered with hair still dark as a raven's wing, and the teeth retaining all their original regularity and whiteness. 'The scene,' we are told, 'was so imposing that most of the workmen stood bare and uncovered, and at the same time felt their frames thrilling with some indefinable emotion as they gazed on the ashes of him whose fame is as wide as the world itself. But the effect was momentary; for when they proceeded to insert a shell or case below the coffin, the head separated from the trunk, and the whole body, with the exception of the bones, crumbled into dust.' Ere yet the advancing morn had empearled the east, the precious relics on which the gloaming of the day and the lamps carried by the

Among "thy Sepulchres Dumfries The Poet's Tomb is there"

party had faintly glimmered, were hid from sight in the darkness of their new tenement.

Not finally, however, as on the night preceding the burial of 'Bonnie Jean' (31st March 1834), the remains of the poet were viewed by a party of gentlemen, including Provost Murray, Mr Archibald Hamilton, writer, Rector M'Millan, Mr James Bogie, Mr Andrew Crombie, builder, Mr John M'Diarmid of the *Courier*, and Dr Archibald Blacklock, who visited the vault in order to obtain a cast of the skull for phrenological purpose. Dr Blacklock in reporting upon the subject states that the cranium was found in a high state of preservation, the bones of the face and palate being also sound; 'and some small portions of black hair with a very few gray hairs intermixed, were observed while detaching some extraneous matter from the occiput.' The skull was carried away to the house of Mr Kerr, plasterer (in North Queensberry Street, now occupied by his son Mr William M'Diarmid Kerr) and a plaster matrix was taken of it by his assistant, Mr James Fraser*, afterwards Bailie Fraser. Two or three tiny tresses that had adhered to the napkin in which the cranium was wrapped were retained, as priceless souvenirs of the illustrious dead. After being a few hours out of the vault the skull was replaced – all the nocturnal operations having been completed as the clock of St Michael's chimed the hour of one.

*A cast of the skull having been transmitted to the Phrenological Society of Edinburgh, Mr George Combe drew up from it a report on the cerebral development of the poet. The cranium was $22^{1}/_{4}$ inches in circumference; from ear to ear vertically over the top of the head, 14 inches; length, 8 inches; greatest breadth, nearly 6. 'These measurements,' says Mr Combe, 'exceed the average of Scotch living heads, *including the integuments*, for which four-eighths of an inch may be allowed.'

William McDowall, 1875–88

Now see where Caledonia's Genius mourns,
And plants the holly round the tomb o' Burns.

On a Schoolmaster In Cleish Parish, Kinross-shire

Here lie Willie Michie's banes;
O Satan, when ye tak him,
Gie him the schoolin' of your weans,
For clever deils he'll mak them!

Robert Burns, 1759–96

Dr John Brown, author of the Brownonian System of Physic, a man of somewhat coarse manners, on passing the monument of David Hume, in the Calton burying-ground, observed to a mason who was laying a pavement stone for it, 'Friend,' said he, 'this is a strong and massy building; but how do you think the honest gentleman can get out at the resurrection?' The mason archly replied, 'Sir, I have secured that point, for I have put the *key under the door*!'

Robert Chambers, 1802–71

Epitaph, Lauder

Alexander Thompson.

Her lyes interred an honest man,
Who did this churchyard first lie in;
This monument shall make it known
That he was the first laid in this ground.
Of mason and of masonrie
He cutted stones right curiously.
To heaven we hope that he is gone,
Where Christ is the Chief Corner Stone.

Epitaph, Dundee

Here lies John, late Mayor of Dundee,
Here lies Him, here lies He,
A. B. C. D. E. F. G.
Di Do Dum, Di, Do, Dee.

Brechin, 1619

The Session considering that monie abuses are admittat in making epitaphs be young men in this citie affixing on burial stanes anie thing they ples, partlie rediculous and partlie ontrew, ordain that no epitaph shall be put on any monuments without the approval of the session.

Journal, 8 October 1827

A wild world, my masters, this Scotland
of ours must have been ...
'For treason, d'ye see,
Was to them a dish of tea,
And murder bread and butter'.

Sir Walter Scott, 1771–1832

Executed lately at Leith:

for 25 years of murder
and cannibalism
Sawney Bean
of Bennane Head, Ballantrae
his wife
his eight sons, his eighteen grandsons
his six daughters, his fourteen
granddaughters
justly dismembered and burned alive.

Records of Argyll

Lord Niel Campbell sent John Grant to Isla *(Ila)* to collect rents. MacLean
of Duart happening to be in Isla at the time, he seized Grant and his rents,
and carried them with him to Duart Castle *(Caisteal Dubhairt)*. When Lord
Niel discovered where his factor was, he went to Dunollie *(Dunolla)* and
said to MacDougall, 'Will you go to Duart for my factor, for it is useless for
me to go on account of the unpleasant terms on which I am with
MacLean?' MacDougall answered that he would. When he reached Duart,
MacLean met him on the shore and saluted him courteously. MacDougall
informed him that he came for Lord Niel's factor. 'Let us dine first,' said
MacLean; 'we can talk of that business afterwards.' After dinner
MacDougall said to MacLean, 'Where is Grant, for it is time for me to set
off homewards?' Upon this MacLean moved to the other side of the room
and said coolly, 'His head is here, but his body is out there, and you can

take it with you if you choose.' MacDougall answered, 'I will take with me what there is of him, since I have come for him.' Grant's body is buried in the churchyard of Kilbrandon *(Cille-bhreanain)*, but his head is in Mull *(Muile)*. John Grant met his fate in 1681, according to his gravestone.

Lord Archibald Campbell, 1846–1913

An essay towards an history and description of Roslyn Chapel, Scotland

At the S E angle of the chapel is a wreathed column ... popularly called *the apprentice's pillar*. A silly story is told respecting this: that the master mason having received a model of a column from abroad, of a very unusual form and character, thought it necessary to inspect the original before he would execute one after the design; during his absence his apprentice finished the pillar, which was much admired. The master on his return heard many praises bestowed on his boy, and in a fit of envious indignation killed him with a hammer. Two heads in this part of the chapel are also said to represent the master and the apprentice. One having a scar or indentation on the forehead, and the other being marked as an old man frowning, and of savage aspect.

John Britton, 1771–1857

The Dowie Dens o' Yarrow, Joseph Noel Paton. NMS

The Dowie Houms o' Yarrow

Late at een, drinkin' the wine,
And ere they paid the lawin',
They set a combat them between,
To fight it in the dawin'.

'O stay at hame, my noble lord!
O stay at hame, my marrow!
My cruel brother will you betray,
On the dowie houms o' Yarrow.'

O fare ye weel, my lady gay!
O fare ye weel, my Sarah!
For I maun gae, tho' I ne'er return
Frae the dowie banks o' Yarrow.'

She kiss'd his cheek, she kamed his hair,
As she had done before, O;
She belted on his noble brand,
An' he's awa to Yarrow.

O he's gane up yon high, high hill –
I wat he gaed wi' sorrow –
An' in a den spied nine arm'd men,
I' the dowie houms o' Yarrow.

'O are ye come to drink the wine,
As ye hae done before, O?
Or are ye come to wield the brand,
On the dowie houms o' Yarrow?

'I am no come to drink the wine,
As I hae done before, O,
But I am come to wield the brand,
On the dowie houms o' Yarrow.'

Four he hurt an' five he slew,
On the dowie houms o' Yarrow
Till that stubborn knight came him behind,
An' ran his body thorrow.

'Gae hame, gae hame, good brother John,
An' tell your sister Sarah
To come an' lift her noble lord,
Who's sleepin' sound on Yarrow.'

She gaed up yon high, high hill –
I wat she gaed wi' sorrow –
An' in a den spied nine dead men,
On the dowie houms o' Yarrow.

She kiss'd his cheek, she kamed his hair,
As oft she did before, O;
She drank the red blood frae him ran,
On the dowie houms o' Yarrow.

Traditional

The House with the Green Shutters

'Where's my hammer?' snarled Gourlay.

'Is it no by the clock?' said his wife wearily. 'Oh, I remember, I remember! I gied it to Mrs Webster to break some brie-stone to rub the front doorstep wi'. It'll be lying in the porch.'

'Oh, ay, as usual,' said Gourlay – 'as usual.'

'John!' she cried in alarm, 'you don't mean to take down the gun, do ye?'

'Huts, you auld fule, what are you skirling for? D'ye think I mean to shoot the dog? Set back on your creepie and make less noise, will ye?'

Ere he had driven a nail in the rafter John came in, and sat down by the fire, taking up the great poker, as if to cover his nervousness. If Gourlay had been on the floor he would have grappled with him there and then. But the temptation to gloat over his victim from his present height was irresistible. He went up another step, and sat down on the very summit of the ladder, his feet resting on one of the lower rounds. The hammer he had been using was lying on his thigh, his hand clutched about its haft.

'Ay, man, you've been taking a bit walk, I hear.'

John made no reply, but played with the poker. It was so huge, owing to Gourlay's whim, that when it slid through his fingers it came down on the muffled hearthstone with a thud like a pavior's hammer.

'I'm told you saw the Deacon on your rounds? Did he compliment you on your return?'

At the quiet sneer a lightning-flash showed John that Allardyce had quizzed him too. For a moment he was conscious of a vast self-pity. 'Damn them, they're all down on me,' he thought. Then a vindictive rage against them all took hold of him, tense, quivering.

'Did you see Thomas Brodie when ye were out?' came the suave inquiry.

'I saw him,' said John, raising fierce eyes to his father's. He was proud of the sudden firmness in his voice. There was not fear in it, no quivering. He was beyond caring what happened to the world or him.

'Oh, you saw him,' roared Gourlay, as his anger leapt to meet the anger of his son. 'And what did he say to you, may I speir? ... Or maybe I should speir what he did ... Eh?' he grinned.

'By God, I'll kill ye,' screamed John, springing to his feet, with the poker in his hand. The hammer went whizzing past his ear. Mrs Gourlay screamed and tried to rise from her chair, her eyes goggling in terror. As Gourlay leapt, John brought the huge poker with a crash on the descending brow. The fiercest joy of his life was the dirl that went up his arm as the steel thrilled to its own hard impact on the bone. Gourlay thudded on the fender, his brow crashing on the rim.

At the blow there had been a cry as of animals from the two women. There followed an eternity of silence, it seemed, and a haze about the place; yet not a haze, for everything was intensely clear; only it belonged to another world. One terrible fact had changed the Universe. The air was different now – it was full of murder. Everything in the room had a new significance, a sinister meaning. The effect was that of an unholy spell.

As through a dream Mrs Gourlay's voice was heard crying on her God.

John stood there, suddenly weak in his limbs, and stared, as if petrified, at the red poker in his hand. A little wisp of grizzled hair stuck to the square of it, severed, as by scissors, between the sharp edge and the bone. It was the sight of that bit of hair that roused him from his stupor – it seemed so monstrous and horrible, sticking all by itself to the poker. 'I didna strike him so hard,' he pleaded, staring vaguely, 'I didna strike him so hard.' Now that the frenzy had left him, he failed to realize the force of his own blow. Then with a horrid fear on him, 'Get up, faither,' he entreated; 'get up, faither! O man, you micht get up!'

Janet, who had bent above the fallen man, raised an ashen face to her brother, and whispered hoarsely, 'His heart has stopped, John; you have killed him!'

Steps were heard coming through the scullery. In the fear of discovery Mrs Gourlay shook off the apathy that held her paralyzed. She sprang up, snatched the poker from her son, and thrust it in the embers.

'Run, John; run for the doctor,' she screamed. – 'O Mrs Webster, Mrs Webster, I'm glad to see ye. Mr Gourlay fell from the top o' the ladder, and smashed his brow on the muckle fender.'

George Douglas Brown, 1869–1902

The Twa Corbies

As I was walking all alane,
I heard twa corbies making a mane:
The tane unto the thither did say,
'Whaur sall we gand and dine the day?'

'In behint yon auld fail dyke
I wot there lies a new-slain knight;
And naebody kens that he lies there
But his hawk, his hound, and his lady fair.

His hound is to the hunting gane,
His hawk to fetch the wild-fowl hame,
His lady's ta'en anither mate,
So we may mak' our dinner sweet.

Ye'll sit on his white hause-bane,
And I'll pike out his bonny blue e'en:
Wi' ae lock o' his gowden hair
We'll theek our nest when it grows bare,

Mony a one him maks mane,
But nane sall ken whar he is gane:
O'er his white banes, when they are bare,
The wind sall blaw for evermair.'

Traditional

Epitaph

Here lies John Kennedy.
If ye saw him noo, ye wadna ken him na.

Mortsafe from Airth, dating from 1831. A mortsafe was fastened over a coffin in a grave as a defence against resurrectionists. NMS

Life of Sir Robert Christison

The time chosen in the dark winter nights was, for the town churchyards, from six to eight o'clock; at which latter hour the churchyard watch was set, and the city police also commenced their night rounds. A hole was dug down to the coffin only where the head lay a canvas sheet being stretched around to receive the earth, and to prevent any of it spoiling the smooth uniformity of the grass. The digging was done with short, flat dagger shaped implements of wood, to avoid the clicking noise of iron striking stones. On reaching the coffin, two broad iron hooks under the lid, pulled forcibly up with a rope broke off a sufficient portion of the lid to allow the body to be dragged out and sacking was heaped over the whole to deaden the sound of the cracking wood. The body was stripped of the grave clothes, which were scrupulously buried again; it was secured in a sack; and the surface of the ground was carefully restored to its original condition, – which was not difficult, as the sod over a fresh-filled grave must always present signs of a recent disturbance. The whole process could be completed in an hour, even though the grave might be six feet deep, because the soil was loose, and the digging was done impetuously by frequent relays of active men. Transference over the churchyard wall was easy in a dark evening – and once in the street, the carrier of the sack drew no attention at so early an hour.

Sir Robert Christison, 1797–1882

Folk Lore and Genealogies of Uppermost Nithsdale

When John Thomson, the son of Dr Thomson, of Sanquhar, was attending his medical classes in Edinburgh he was shocked one day to see on the dissecting table the body of a man whom he knew well, and who had been buried in Sanquhar kirkyard only a few days previously.

The resurrection business was carried on in quite a wholesale fashion; and, in some instances, with but little attempt at concealment. One fine summer day, when the weavers and other workmen had finished their mid-day meal, and were standing in groups on the street, enjoying a smoke, and talking over the news of the day, a gig with a lady and gentleman drove into the town from the west, passed down the street, and pulled up a the inn at the Townfoot, tenanted by Andrew Lamont. Handing the reins to a boy, the man got out, and entering the inn ordered a glass of whisky, which he drank standing. A bystander passed a remark upon the fine weather they were then having, enquired whether the stranger and travelled far, and further ventured to ask if he was not going to treat his goodwife to a dram. To these queries the traveller replied that he had come from Ayrshire, and that his wife never took spirits; and, bidding his interrogator good-day, reseated himself beside the lady in the trap. Now while the stranger was in the inn some of the weavers come forward to have a look at the turnout, the gig being particularly smart looking, and the horse a fine, dashing animal. The lady, heavily veiled, and with a plaid drawn round her, sat erect in the trap. A certain stiffness about her posture, however, caused some curiosity among the onlookers, which was increased when the man got in beside her; for she made not the slightest movement when he got in, but sat bolt erect, and when the horse made a move fell slightly forward. Then it was discovered that a rope was passed round her body fastening her to the back of the seat.

A shout immediately got up that it was a corpse the man had beside him, and a rush was made for the gig. But, putting his whip to the horse, the stranger quickly got away, and the steed dashed down the street at a full gallop. The weavers made after him, others further on joined the chase, and one man made a bold attempt to get hold of the horse; but lashing out with his whip at his assailant, the resurrection man got safely away. Who he was, where he had come from, and whither he was going with his ghastly companion was never found out.

William Wilson, 1830–1908

Burke and Hare

Down the close and up the stair,
But and ben wi' Burke and Hare.
Burke's the butcher, Hare's the thief,
Knox's the man who buys the beef.

Traditional

A full and Particular account of the Execution of W BURKE, who was hanged at Edinburgh on Wednesday the 28th January, 1829; also, an account of his conduct and behaviour since his condemnation, and on the Scaffold.

Early on Wednesday morning, the Town of Edinburgh was filled with an immense croud of spectators, from all places of the surrounding country, to witness the execution of a Monster, whose crime stands unparalleled in the annals of Scotland: viz – for cruelly murdering Margery M'Conegal, and afterwards selling her body to the Doctors in October last.

Whilst this unhappy man was under sentence, he made the following Confession: – that he had been engaged in this murderous traffic from Christmas 1827, until the murder of the woman Docherty, or M'Conegal, in October last; during which period, he had butchered Sixteen of his fellow-creatures, and that he had no accomplice but Hare, – that they perpetrated these fearful atrocities by suffocation. When they succeeded in making their victims drunk, the one held the mouth and nostrils, whilst the other went upon the body, and in this manner was the woman Docherty killed; they then sold her body to Doctor — in his rooms, and

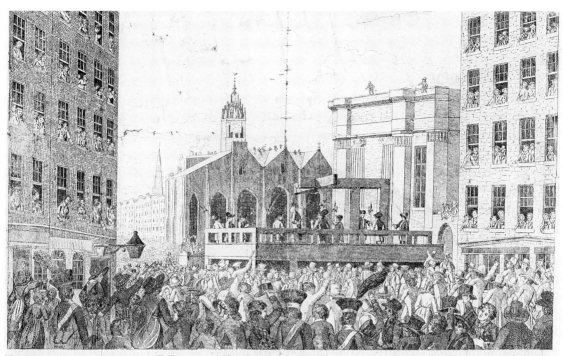

EXECUTION of the notorious WILLIAM BURKE the murderer, who supplied DR KNOX with subjects.

Execution of William Burke. City of Edinburgh Art Centre

received payment at his house and that they were never Resurrectionists; all the bodies they sold being murdered, except one, who died a natural death in Hare's house.

At an early hour on Tuesday, he was taken in a coach from the jail on the Calton Hill to the Lock-up, a prison immediately adjacent to the place of execution. He spent the day in silence, reading, and devotion, and on Tuesday night he slept soundly for several hours. About seven o'clock, the two Catholic clergymen arrived, and were admitted to the cell, and they were soon after followed by the Rev Mr Marshall. The religious ceremonies being performed, he talked firmly, declared that death had not terrors, and expressed a hope of pardon and happiness. During the night, Burke stated that he was happy, that he had at last been arrested in his career of crime, and brought to justice. Though he had been a great offender, yet he rested on the atonement of the Saviour for salvation. When the irons were knocked off, he exclaimed, 'Thank God these are off, and all will be off shortly.' Shortly after eight o'clock, the procession set out for the place of execution. Bailies Crichton and Small, with a party of town officers, first ascended the scaffold, and they were followed by Burke, supported by the two Catholic Clergymen. He was dressed in decent black clothes, and was perfectly firm and composed. The moment he appeared, the crowd set up an appalling shout, which continued for several minutes. The murderer and the Catholic clergymen then knelt down and spent a few minutes in devotion, and the religious exercises were concluded by a prayer from the Rev Mr Marshall. As soon as the executioner proceeded to do his duty, the cries of 'Burke him, Burke him, give him no rope,' and many others of a similar complexion were vociferated in voices loud with indignation. Burke, in the mean time, stood perfectly unmoved, and gazed around till the cap was drawn over his face, and shut the world for ever from his view.

The executioner having completed his preparations and placed the signal in Burke's hand, the magistrates, ministers and attendants left the scaffold. The crowd again set up another long and loud cheer, which was followed by cries for 'Hare, Hare!', 'Where is Hare?' 'Hang Hare!' and so on. Burke lifted his hands and ejaculated a prayer of a few sentences – then dropt the napkin, and momently the drop fell. The struggle was neither long nor apparently severe; but at every convulsive motion, a loud huzza arose from the multitude, which was several times repeated even after the last agonies of humanity were past. During the time of the wretched man's suspension, not a single indication of pity was observable among the vast crowd – on the contrary, every countenance wore the lively aspect of a gala day, while puns and jokes on the occasion were freely bandied about, and produced bursts of laughter and merriment, which were not confined to the juvenile spectators alone. '*Burke* Hare too!' 'Wash blood from the land!' 'One cheer more!' and similar exclamations, were repeated in different directions, until the culprit was cut down, about nine o'clock, when one general and tremendous huzza closed the awful exhibition – and the multitude immediately thereafter began to disperse.

Burke's body is to be dissected, and his Skeleton to be preserved, in order that posterity may keep in remembrance his atrocious crimes.

PRICE ONE PENNY.

Recollections of a Speyside Parish

The watch-house is associated in the writer's memory with a host of incidents that left a deep impression of the horrible deeds done by resurrectionists. Few at the present day can remember the agitation caused in Scotland when the dreadful deeds and doings of Burke and Hare were made public. Horror and dread became epidemic, and the whole country

Corpse collar, or mort collar, from Kingskettle, Fife. This was bolted through the bottom of the coffin and round the neck of the corpse, to prevent its theft by resurrectionists. NMS

was in a fever of agitation at the thought of having the remains of a wife, a mother, or father dragged from the grave and carried off to some dreadful den, there to be hacked and mutilated like a beast. The very thought of such a thing roused the people in many places to desperation. In Aberdeen they demolished the Surgeon's Hall, for they looked upon that detested place as little better than a shambles, where human bodies were bought, like dead beasts, according to their value. The stories told at that time of the deeds done in that human slaughter-house are too horrible to relate. There is little doubt that few of them had any foundation in fact, but they were the means of rousing the deepest feelings of a people who had a great reverence and respect for their dead. They rose up, determined to baulk the resurrectionists of their prey. A watch-house was erected in many graveyards; indeed, very few in the north-eastern counties were without an erection of some kind to shelter the watchers of the dead, and their ruins may be seen in many graveyards at the present day.

A short description of a watch-house well remembered by the writer may interest the reader. The one referred to was built of rough stones, and was about ten feet square. It stood on a spot that overlooked the whole of the graveyard. On either side of the door was a narrow slit or window, that opened and closed with strong wooden shutters. Through these apertures the watchers could reconnoitre unobserved, and, if need be, fire their guns upon the desecrators of the grave. The fire-place was opposite the door, and over it hung two claymores that had done service at Culloden; upon a small table in the centre of the apartment lay an open Bible, a snuff-mull, pipes, and a bottle of Usqubae also stood there to refresh the weary watchers. Had the staunchest teetotaller been there, he would have been sorely tempted to fill the quaich and taste the contents of the bottle. Few at the present time have any idea of the hardships entailed upon the male population of a small parish, in having to watch over the remains of their friends and neighbours for six weeks. That was the prescribed time necessary. The watch-house in some cases was occupied the whole of the winter months, if an epidemic was prevalent in the parish.

One dark November night ... Jamie Gordon and Johnny Dustan 'watched the dead.' Owing to the darkness of the night, they were obliged to leave the watch-house and survey the ground, lantern in hand. Jamie Gordon undid the bolt, lifted the latch, and was in the act of stepping out, when lo! in a moment he was upset, overturning the table, and the lamp and lantern were both extinguished. Jamie fought manfully with the beast, for they could see by the dim light of the fire that it was a beast of some kind that they were contending with; but all in vain. They were both vanquished, thrown down, and trodden upon by what they believed to be an evil spirit in the shape of a beast, conjured, no doubt, by the departed witch in revenge for the disrespect shown to her remains by a section of the parishioners. Johnny Dustan, more self-possessed than his companion, called out, 'Sain yersel', Jamie; we're in the pooer o' the enemy. God gi'e us a gweed reddance.' How they escaped the fury of the beast and came to the village they were never able to tell. When morning dawned, everyone hastened to the kirkyard to see and hear all particulars. Every hole and corner were examined, but no explanation could be found of the strange occurrence, until daft Jock Flemin' called out from a distant corner of the graveyard, 'Ye're a' feels thegither; Tibbie's quiet enough in her lair. Here's the beast that beat ye baith.' And there, sure enough, lay Duncan Macpherson's ram beneath a gravestone!

James Thomson, c1825–1907

Letter to Joshua Brookes, 1825

There are plenty of subjects to be got here in the Highlands, for there are churchyards without churches and very distant from any house. I should suppose also that from the great bodily exertion which the Highlanders

The ancient burial place at Keills. Alasdair Alpin MacGregor.

are accustomed to, in climbing their mountains, they will be capital subjects for demonstrating the muscles. Besides, the facility afforded for conveyance by steamboats is such that nothing would be more easy than to supply the whole London school from this quarter.

Skye: Iochdar-Trotternish

A church once existed at Sartle, dedicated to Saint Maolrubha. The usual graveyard was beside, or contained it, called Cill-Maree. All those cills have been walled in recently. An old man described this as a waste of money. 'Does any want to go there, and can anyone there come out?'

William Mackenzie, 1851–1935

Life and Times of Rev John Wightman, DD, of Kirkmahoe

In the second session of the first Parliament of James VII, held at Edinburgh, 1686, an Act was passed called the 'Act for Burying in Scots Linen,' in which it was ordained, for the encouragement of the linen manufactures within the kingdom, that no person whatsoever, of high or low degree, should be buried in any shirt, sheet, or anything else, except in plain linen or cloth, of Hards made and spun within the kingdom, and without lace or point. There was specially prohibited the use of Holland, or other linen cloth made in other kingdoms; and of silk, woollen, gold, or silver, or any other stuff than what was made of Hards spun and wrought within the kingdom, under the penalty of 300 pounds Scots for a nobleman, and 200 pounds for every other person for each offence. One-half of this penalty was to go to the informer, and the other half to the poor of the parish of where the body should be interred. And, for the better discovery of contraveners, it was ordained that every minister within the kingdom should keep an account and register of all persons buried in his parish. A certificate upon oath, in writing, duly attested by two 'famous' persons, was to be delivered by one of the relatives to the minister within eight days, declaring that the deceased person had been shrouded in the manner prescribed; which certificate was to be recorded without charge. The penalty was to be sued for by the minister before any judge competent; and if he should prove negligent in pursuing the contraveners within six months after the interment, he himself was liable for the said fine.

Rev David Hogg, 1815–79

Folk Lore

The reasons given for watching the corpse differed in different localities. The practice is still observed, I believe, in some places; but probably now it is more the result of habit – a custom followed without any basis of definite belief, and merely as a mark of respect for the dead; but in former times, and within this century, it was firmly held that if the corpse were not watched, the devil would carry off the body, and many stories were current of such an awful result having happened. One such story was told me by a person who had received the story from, a person who was present at the wake where the occurrence happened ... The corpse was laid out in a room, and the watchers had retired to another apartment to partake of refreshments, having shut the door of the room where the corpse lay. While they were eating there was heard a great noise, as of a struggle between two persons, proceeding from the room where the corpse lay. None of the party would venture into the room, and in this emergency they sent for the minister, who came, and, with the open Bible in his hand, entered the room and shut the door. The noise then ceased, and in about ten minutes he came out, lifted the tongs from the fireplace, and again re-entered the room. When he came out again, he brought out with the tongs a glove, which was seen to be bloody, and this he put into the fire. He refused, however, to tell either what he had seen or heard; but on the watchers returning to their post, the corpse lay as formerly, and as quiet and unruffled as if nothing had taken place, whereat they were all surprised.

James Napier, 1810–84

Social Life in Scotland

Captain Burt supplies these particulars: 'After the death of anyone, not in the lowest circumstances, the friends and acquaintances of the deceased, assemble to keep the relations company in the first night; and they dance, as if it were at a wedding, till the next morning, though all the time the corpse lies before them, in the same room. If the deceased be a woman, the widower leads up the first dance; if a man, the widow. But this Highland custom, I knew to my disturbance, within less than a quarter of a mile of Edinburgh, before I had been among the mountains. It was upon the death of a smith, next door to my lodgings, who was a Highlander.'

At the funeral of William Alexander, seaman, who died at Alloa in 1725, these items were incurred:

Twentie pints eall [ale], £13 6 0
Two pints aquavitae [whisky], 2 0 0
Bread [shortbread], 2 3 0
Tobacco and pipes, 0 10 0
Four pound chees, 0 12 0

These mortuary festivities were relished not only by the living, but the departed comforted their later hours by contemplating their occurrence. Dean Ramsay relates that an aged spinster lady in Strathspey, when she was on her deathbed, called to her bedside her grand-nephew and heir, and affectionately charged him that as much whisky was to be used at her funeral as had been drunk at her baptism. Unaware as to the extent of the potations on the earlier occasion, the heir allowed each one who attended the funeral to drink what he pleased. The result was a

contretemps which the aged gentlewoman could not have foreseen without emotion. When the funeral party reached the churchyard, a distance of ten miles from the place of starting, the sexton's enquiry of the chief mourner, 'Captain, whaur's Miss Kitty?' aroused the company to the recollection that in resting at an inn they had there left the body on a dyke, and had started without it.' In connection with the Lord President Forbes a similar incident occurred. At his mother's funeral he entertained his neighbours with such profuse hospitality, that he and his friends were startled on reaching the churchyard by the discovery that the coffin had been forgotten. At the funeral of the Hon. Alexander Fraser of Lovat in 1815, several persons overcome with liquor fell into the vault; and the carousals which in 1817 attended the funeral of the Chisholm were accompanied with some fatal incidents.

Funeral festivities have led to strife, even to fatal conflicts. At a funeral procession at Meigle, in 1707, David Ogilvie of Clunie, quarrelling by the way with his neighbour, Andrew Couper, younger of Lochblair, discharged a pistol at him, when he fell from his horse mortally wounded. Ogilvie who was thoroughly inebriated, was sheltered for some weeks by the writer's great-grandfather, who resided in the district. Thereafter he found shelter in France.

Charles Rogers, 1825–1890

Records of Argyll

The excesses indulged in by the natives of Tiree (*Tirithe*) at funerals in bygone days caused the then factor, Colonel Campbell, to enact a law that only three rounds should be allowed to be given to those at the funeral – a round meaning a glassful of spirits. Previously it used to be nine rounds. At the first funeral after this enactment, that of Gilleaspuig Làidir (Strong Archie), or Archie M'Lean, Kilmoluaig (*Cill-malnaig*), his son came to the Colonel and asked liberty, as it was the first, to be allowed to give the usual allowance, or at least that he would not be confined to the exact *three*. The Colonel was unmoved, and would not allow his laws to be broken as soon as made. The son went home quite downhearted at the disgrace and dishonour he was compelled to submit to. A happy idea came to his head, by which he would be able to show respect to both the living and the dead – viz, he got two bull's horns, corked at the one end, and made so as to hold three glassfuls. He gave three rounds of the horns; and thus the Colonel's laws were observed, and his father buried with the usual nine glasses apiece to each at the funeral.

Lord Archibald Campbell, 1846–1913

Report of the Funeral on 11 June 1635 of the Earl of Buccleuch from *Domestic Annals of Scotland*

A striking sight it must have been, that long heraldic procession which went before the body of the deceased noble, along the banks of the Teviot, on that bright June day. First there were forty-six *saulies* in black gowns and hoods, with black staves in the hands, headed by one called a conductor, who was attended by an old man in a mourning gown; a trumpeter in the Buccleuch livery following, and sounding his trumpet. Next came

Illustrations recording the funeral ceremonies of the Duke of Rothes, 1681. NMS

Robert Scott of Howshaw, fully armed, riding on a fair horse, and carrying on the point of a lance a little banner of the defunct's colours, azure and or. Then a horse in black, led by a lackey in mourning, a horse with a crimson velvet foot-mantle, and 'three trumpets in mourning on foot, sounding sadly'. Then the great gumpheon, of black taffeta carried on a lance by Walter Scott of Lauchope, his sword borne by Andrew Scott of Broadmeadows, his gauntlets by Francis Scott of Castleside, and his coat of honour by Mr Lawrence Scott.

The next great section of the procession was a purely heraldic display. Eight gentlemen of the Clan Scott bore each the coat of arms of one of

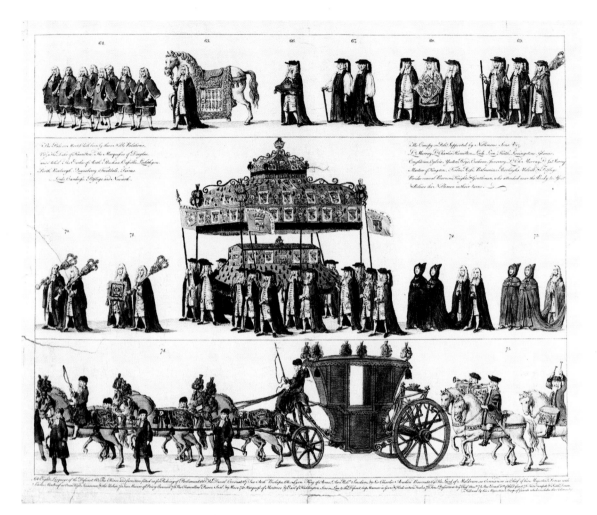

the various paternal and maternal ancestors of the defunct. Other gentlemen of the name – Scott of Harden, Scott of Scotstarvet, etc – carried the great pencil, the deceased's standard, his coronet, and his 'arms in metal and colour', near whom were three more trumpets and three pursuivants, all in mourning. 'Last of all came the corps, carried under a fair pall of black velvet, decked with arms, larmes (tears), and cipress of sattin, knopt with gold, and on the coffin the defunct's helmet and coronet, overlaid with cipress, to shew that he was a soldier. And so in this order, with the conduct of many honourable friends, marched they from Branxholm to Hawick Church, where after the funeral sermon ended, the corps were interred amongst his ancestors.'

Robert Chambers, 1802–71, quoting Sir James Balfour

Macabre invitation to a funeral in Greyfriars Churchyard, 1739. NMS

The Oliphants of Gask

The House of Gask, once filled to overflowing, became stiller as the years went on, and the sons and daughters went out into life one after another. In 1729 the wife, Janet Murray, died. In the handwriting of Laurence Oliphant, the younger, is a closely written list of goods ordered for his mother's funeral. These include 'a dozen lobsters, three large cods and a few small fish of what kinds can be gott, and a dozen of habets, if it is possible to gett a few oysters or crabs.'

These were to come from Crail. From Edinburgh he ordered anchovies, capers, olives, bottles cucumbers, 'six forren mangoes,' a mutchkin of walnuts, a pot of barberries, seven hundred pickled oysters, six neats tongues, a 'mutchkin of sweet oyll,' two pounds of 'marmallit of oranges,' spices, sweets, 'half a pound of truffles and the same of morells,' 'and a chopen bottle of good snuff.'

He also gives an order, 'That the room be hung of black garge and the Kirk seats and pulpit. That ye Isle be plaistered and painted black, with white tears, also the ston room doors and windows and the door of the church.'

The amount of food was astonishing. For meat there was a hind leg of fine beef from Perth, a fine veal, a cow to be killed at Gask, a roast of pork, four muttons, two dozen choice hens, six capons. The drink supplied included ten dozen of strong claret, five dozen small, two dozen chirrey, two dozen brandy, a barrel of brandy. Knives, forks and spoons were bought, and six dozen wine glasses, but the extra chairs required were borrowed from Lord Rollo and from Millearne. The Charley Murrays lent a cook to help the Gask and Williamston cooks.

Laurence ordered for his father's mourning, 'A mourning night-gown and bell for Gask and a black big coat, and a hole of sadle furniture covered with black.' His mourning cost £2, 2s. Scots, but this included 'black for the chaplain, crape for the servants' hatts etc.'

E Maxtone Graham d 1952

Carved pine panel of the heraldic achievement of Henrietta Mordaunt, widow of the second Duke of Gordon (between 1728 and 1760), from a pew in St Paul's Church, Aberdeen. NMS

From *The Testament of Mr Andro Kennedy*

> *In die mee sepulture*
> I will nane haif bot our awne gyng,
> *Et duos rusticos de rure*
> Berand a berell on a styng;
> Drynkand and playand cop out, evin,
> *Sicut egomet solebam;*
> Singand and playand with hie stevin
> *Potum meum cum fletu miscebam.*
>
> I will na preistis for me sing
> *Dies illa, Dies ire;*

Na yit na bellis for me ring,
Sicut semper solet fieri;
Bot a bag pipe to play a spryng,
Et unum ail wosp ante me
In stayd of baneris for to bring;
Quatuor lagenas cervisie,
Within the graif to set sic thing
In modum crucis juxta me,
To fle the fendis, than hardely sing
De terra plasmasti me.

William Dunbar, 1460–c1513

Coffin pall decoration in oil on black silk with the arms of Alexander, fourth Duke of Gordon, 1827. NMS

Galloway funeral. John Copland

Scottish Reminiscences

My grannie was weel kent to be no' canny. She had ways of doin' things and kennin' things that naebody could mak oot. At last she deeit, and she behoved to be buryit i' the Barr, that's a village on the ither side o' the hills, laigh doon by the Stinchar. When the funeral day cam', we carryit the coffin up the steep road, and when we were gettin' near the tap, and hadna mickle breath left, for the coffin was nae licht wecht, a fine-lookin' gentleman, ridin' a fine black horse, made up to us. Nane o' us kennt him or had seen him afore. But he rade alangside o' us, and cracked awa' maist croosely, and cheered us sae that we gaed scrievin' doon the brae on the ither side. Weel, you may jalouse we were a wee bit forfeuchen when we cam' to the kirkyard, and some o' us thocht we wadna be the waur o' bit drappie afore we gaed on wi' the buryin'. Sae we steppit into the pub-lic-hoose. Weel, ye mauna think we bydeit lang there, but losh me! when we cam' oot the coffin wi' my grannie in't was awa', and sae was the man an' the black horse. And to this day I canna tell what cam' ower them.

Archibald Geikie, 1835–1924

The body lay on the bed in the best room; it had on a shirt well ruffled, a night cap, and the hands were crossed over the breast. A white sheet was spread over all, white napkins were pinned down on all the chair cushions, spread over the chest of drawers and the tables, and pinned over the few prints hung on the walls. Two bottles of wine and a plate of seed cake were on one small table, bread, cheese, butter, and whiskey on another, offered according to the rank of the numerous visitors by the one solitary watcher beside the corpse, a decent comely woman, a natural daughter of the poor Captain's who was respectably married to a farmer in Strathspey. A great crowd was gathered in and about the house; the name of each new arrival was carried up immediately to Mrs Grant, who bowed her head in approbation; the more that came the higher the compliment. She said nothing, however, she had a serious part to play – the highland Widow, and most decorously she went through it. Every body expected it from her, for when had she ever failed in any duty; and every body must have been gratified, for this performance was faultless. She sat on the Captain's cornered arm chair in a spare bedroom, dressed in a black gown, and with a white handkerchief pinned on her head, one side pinned round the head, and then all the rest hanging over it like, I must repeat myself, 'the kerchief on the head of some of the prints of our Henry of Bolingbroke.' Motionless the Widow sat during the whole length of the day, silent and motionless. If addressed, she either slowly nodded or waved her head, or, if an answer were indispensible, whispered it. Her insignia of office, the big bright bunch of large house keys, beside her, and if required, a lady friend, first begging permission, and ascertaining by the nod or the wave which key was the proper one, carried off the bunch, gave out what was wanted, and then replaced it. All the directions for the funeral were taken from herself in the same solemn manner. We were quite awe struck, the room was full, crowded up by comers and goers, and yet a pin could have been heard to drop in it. The short question solemnly asked in the lowest tone audible, the dignified sign in reply, alone broke the stillness of the scene – for scene it was. Early in the morning, before company hours, who had been so busy as the Widow. Streaking the corpse, dressing its chamber, settling her own, giving out every bit and every drop that was to be used upstairs and down by gentle and simple, preparing the additional supplies in case of need afterwards so quietly applied for by the friendly young lady, there was nothing, from the merest trifle to the matter of most importance, that she had not, her own active self, seen to.

Elizabeth Grant of Rothiemurchus, 1797–1885

'But, Ailsie Gourlay, ye're the auldest o' us three, did ye ever see a mair grand bridal?'

'I winna say that I have,' answered the hag; 'but I think soon to see as braw a burial.'

'And that wad please me as weel,' said Annie Winnie; 'for there's as large a dole, and folk are no obliged to girn and laugh, and mak murgeons, and wish joy to these hellicat quality, that lord it ower us like brute beasts. I like to pack the dead-dole in my lap, and rin ower my auld rhyme, –

My loaf in my lap, my penny in my purse,
 Thou art ne'er the better, and I'm ne'er the worse.'

'That's right, Annie,' said the paralytic woman; 'God send us a green Yule and a fat kirkyard!'

'But I wad like to ken, Lucky Gourlay, for ye're the auldest and wisest amang us, whilk o' these revellers' turns it will be to be streekit first?'

'D'ye see yon dandilly maiden,' said Dame Gourlay 'a' glistenin' wi' goud and jewels, that they are lifting upon the white horse behind that harebrained callant in scarlet, wi' the lang sword at his side?'

'But that's the bride!' said her companion, her cold heart touched with some sort of compassion; 'that's the very bride herself! Eh, whow! sae young, sae braw, and sae bonny – and is her time sae short?'

'I tell ye,' said the sibyl, 'her winding sheet is up as high as her throat already, believe it wha list. Her sand has but a few grains to rin out, and nae wonder – they've been weel shaken. The leaves are withering fast on the trees, but she'll never see the Martinmas wind gar them dance in swirls like the fairy rings.'

Sir Walter Scott, 1771–1832

Epitaph, Loch Ranza

Here lies Donald and his wife
Janet Mac Fee:
Aged 40 he
And 30 she.

The Dowie Dens o' Yarrow, Joseph Noel Paton. NMS

Flora MacDonald

When Flora MacDonald died in Kingsburgh in 1790, her funeral was the largest ever seen in Skye. When the bearers of the coffin came to a swollen stream, they hesitated. One of the mourners cried out 'An e sin a' ? mhisneach a chleachd ise tha sibh ag giùlan?' 'Is that the courage shown by her whom you are carrying?'

The bearers plunged into the torrent.

Traditional

A good wife

Two golfers were on their way home from the links in Fife, when they met a funeral. As the cortege passed by, Alex took off his cap. 'What's up with you,' asked Tom, 'you never usually bother with that.'

'Ach, well' said Alex, 'she was a good wife to me.'

Traditional

The graveyard watch

The person last buried had to keep watch over the graveyard till the next funeral came. This was called *Faire Chlaidh*, the graveyard watch, kept by the spirits of the departed.

Traditional

Confessions of a Justified Sinner

It so happened, that two young men, William Shiel and W Sword, were out, on an adjoining height, this summer, casting peats, and it came into their heads to open this grave in the wilderness, and see if there were any of the bones of the suicide of former ages and centuries remaining. They did so, but opened only one half of the grave, beginning at the head and about the middle at the same time. It was not long till they came upon the old blanket – I think they said not much more than a foot from the surface. They tore that open, and there was the hay rope lying stretched down alongst his breast, so fresh that they saw at first sight that it was made of *risp*, a sort of long sword-grass that grows about marshes and the sides of lakes. One of the young men seized the rope and pulled by it,

Glencorse Church and churchyard. Alasdair Alpin MacGregor

but the old enchantment of the devil, remained, – it would not break; and so he pulled and pulled at it, till behold the body came up into a sitting posture, with a broad blue bonnet on his head, and its plaid around it, all as fresh as that day it was laid in! I never heard of a preservation so wonderful, if it be true as was related to me, for still I have not had the curiosity to go and view the body myself. The features were all so plain, that an acquaintance might easily have known him. One of the lads gripped the face of the corpse with his finger and thumb, and the cheeks felt quite soft and fleshy, but the dimples remained and did not spring out again. He had fine yellow hair, about nine inches long; but not a hair of it could they pull out till they cut part of it off with a knife. They also cut off some portions of his clothes, which were all quite fresh, and distributed them among their acquaintances sending a portion to me, among the rest, to keep as natural curiosities. Several gentlemen have in a manner forced me to give them fragments of these enchanted garments: I have, however, retained a small portion for you, which I send along with this, being a piece of his plaid, and another of his waistcoat breast, which you will see are still as fresh as that day they were laid in the grave.

His broad blue bonnet was sent to Edinburgh several weeks ago, to the great regret of some gentlemen connected with the land, who wished to have it for a keep sake. For my part, fond as I am of blue bonnets, and broad ones in particular, I declare I durst not have worn that one. There was nothing of the silver knife and fork discovered, that I heard of, nor was it very likely it should: but it would appear he had been very near run of cash, which I daresay had been the cause of his utter despair; for, on searching his pockets, nothing was found but three old Scots halfpennies. These young men meeting with another shepherd afterwards, his curiosity was so much excited that they went and digged up the curious remains a second time, which was a pity, as it is likely that by these exposures to the air, and from the impossibility of burying it up again as closely as it was before, the flesh will now fall to dust.

James Hogg, 1770–1835

Notes on the Folk-Lore of the North-East of Scotland

Peculiar horror was manifested towards suicides. Such were not buried in the churchyard. It is not much over half a century since a fierce fight took place in a churchyard in the middle of Banff-shire, to prevent the burial of a suicide in it. By an early hour all the strong men of the parish who were opposed to an act so sacrilegious were astir and hastening to the churchyard with their weapons of defence – strong sticks. The churchyard was taken possession of and the walls manned. The gate and more accessible parts of the wall were assigned to picked men. In due time the suicide's coffin appeared, surrounded by an excited crowd, for the most part armed with sticks. Some, however, carried spades sharpened on the edge. Fierce and long was the fight at the gate, and not a few rolled in the dust. The assailing party was beaten off. A grave was dug outside the churchyard, close beneath the wall, and the coffin laid in it. The lid was lifted, and a bottle of vitriol poured over the body. Before the lid could be again closed, the fumes of the dissolving body were rising thickly over the heads of actors and spectators. This was done to prevent the body from being lifted during the coming night from its resting place, conveyed back to its abode when in life, and placed against the door, to fall at the feet of the member of the family that was the first to open the door in the morning.

Rev Walter Gregor, 1825–97

Notes on the Folk-Lore of the North-East of Scotland

There is a great reluctance in burying the first body in a new graveyard, and as great a reluctance in leaving the old churchyard after a beginning of a burying has been made in the new one. It is told that, when a graveyard on the east coast of Aberdeenshire had to be in a great measure closed, nothing would induce the inhabitants of one of the villages of the parish to bury their dead in the new one. What was to be done? A shoemaker, whose shop was the meeting-place of many of the people of the village, was equal to the difficulty. One night, when a few of the villagers were in the shop, the shoemaker announced that there were 'yird swine' in the old graveyard. All were aroused, but hoped that what the shoemaker said might be a mistake. 'No mistake,' said the man, 'I can show you one that was got in the very place.' The cry was 'Lat's see 't.' A water rat was produced. 'An' that's a yird swine, is't, the creatir it eats the dead bodies?' said the men, standing at a distance, and looking in horror on the abhorred beast. 'Aye, that's the real yird-swine.' The news spread like fire through the village, and many visited the shop to convince themselves of the dreadful truth. The fate of the old graveyard was sealed in that village.

Rev Walter Gregor, 1825–97

Tomb in Greyfriars Churchyard. Alasdair Alpin MacGregor

The Traill family with Greyfriars Bobby. SEA, NMS

The Scotsman 17 January 1872

GREYFRIARS' BOBBY: many will be sorry to hear that the poor but interesting dog, Greyfriars' Bobby, died on Sunday evening. Every kind attention was paid to him in his last days by his guardian, Mr Traill, who has had him buried in a flower-plot near Greyfriars' church. His collar, a gift from the Lord Provost Chambers, has been deposited in the office at the church gate. Mr Brodie, we understand has successfully modelled the figure of Greyfriars' Bobby, which is to surmount the very handsome memorial to be erected by the munificence of the Baroness Burdett-Coutts.

The Scotsman 2 August 1934

As an old Edinburgh citizen I have been greatly interested in the recent references to Greyfriars' Bobby, culminating in your excellent article today.

In 1868 and 1869 I often had the pleasure of seeing Bobby leaving the churchyard to get his dinner. The scene was, of course, a daily occurrence. Towards one o'clock people would gather just outside the large entrance gates, forming a line on each side of the sloping causeway. So widespread was the interest that every class of society was represented, from the well-to-do and fashionably dressed to the artisan and the humble message-boy. As the hour drew near there was a hush of expectation. Then bang went the gun in the Castle, and every head turned to the gate, knowing that at the signal Bobby would break his lonely vigil and set off on the way out. Soon there was a hushed whisper, 'Here he comes!' and the grey, shaggy little figure appeared, pattering over the causeway between the two lines of people. Looking neither to one side not the other, intent only on his own affairs, Bobby hurried round the corner to his right, up the street a few yards, and disappeared into Mr Traill's Dining Rooms for the meal he never failed to get for many years.

By those who cared to wait long enough, his return could also be seen. His dinner finished in reasonable time, the devoted dog, with no interval for idle frolics, returned once more to the grave of his master.

Andrew Hislop, Edinburgh

The Accounts of the Magdalen Chapel, Cowgate, Edinburgh, 1685

Paid John Moffat (the officer) an account for coals and ale furnished by him by the Deacon's orders to the late Alexander Ramsay when his corpse was brought into the Magdalene Chapel and laid before a great fire to see if he would come alive with the heat, in regard he died suddenly, £2,2s.

Received for the late Earl of Argyll's corpse staying in the Chapel, £29 Scots. Spent when I received the £29 for the Earl of Argyll's corpse ten shillings.

(The Ninth Earl of Argyll was executed for treason in 1685.)

Dead-thraws from *The Scottish Gallovidian Encyclopedia*

To the man of feeling, there is not a more horrible sight to be seen, as a fellow creature in this wretched state; how alive we are then to the power of death, and how grieved to the soul that we can render no relief. I was never able to stand the scene but once, and will never try it again, unless abruptly compelled. I do not think death itself will be more difficult for me to endure than that appalling scene was. Once too, that restless being within me, Curiosity, dragged me to see the execution of a young man, when in Edinburgh, but she'll drag well if she drags me back again to see such a spectacle. I was not myself, Mactaggart, for a month afterwards, my mind was so disordered with the sight. In a curious way wrought the phrenzy (as I am one who speaks my mind), I tell this. I felt an inclination, both during night, when dream after dream whirled through my brain's airy halls, and in the day-time, to do some crime or other, that I might meet with a similar fate. Whether this is ever the way with any other person, I cannot tell, but so it operated on me, and which has caused me ever since to say, that *hanging*, instead of scaring from crime, has a strong tendency the other way. May God keep me far from seeing again any in the *dead-throws*.

John MacTaggart, 1797–1830

Glasgow Courier 16 April 1803

Wanted, for the City of Glasgow, an Executioner. The bad character of the person who last held the office having brought on it a degree of discredit which it by no means deserves, the Magistrates are determined to accept of none but a sober well-behaved man. The emoluments are considerable.

Sunday Times 5 January 1834
Emoluments for the Inverness hangman

First, he was provided with a house, bed and bedding.
Second he was allowed 36 peats weekly from the tacksman of the petty customs.
Third, he had a bushel of coals out of every cargo of English coals imported into the town.
Fourth, he was allowed a piece of coal, as large as he could carry, out of every·cargo of Scotch coals.

Fifth, he had a peck of oatmeal out of every hundred bolls landed at the shore.

Sixth, he had a fish from every creel or basket of fish brought to the market.

Seventh, he had a penny for every sack of oatmeal sold at the market.

Eighth, he had a peck of salt out of every cargo.

Ninth, he was allowed every year a suit of clothes, two shirts, two pair of stockings, a hat, and two pair of shoes.

Added to these fixed and regular sources of income, [he] levied black mail on the lieges in the shape of Christmas boxes, and had besides a sum of 5 l. at every execution at which he presided.

The Maiden, the instrument used for beheading criminals in Edinburgh. Constructed in 1564, it was decommissioned in 1710. NMS

The Times 28 March 1856

John Murdoch, who, until disabled by age and infirmity about four years ago, had officiated for a lengthened period as the finisher of the law in Glasgow, and who was the last hangman who is ever likely to be in the ordinary pay of the corporation, has himself at length 'shuffled off this mortal coil.' For a period of above 20 years his stalwart form and grim visage (partially concealed by an old high-necked waterproof) were seen as the presiding genius at every scaffold which was created throughout Scotland, and at not a few in the north of England. Murdoch, who was a baker, came to Glasgow from the north upwards of 20 years since, and was even then advanced in life. He was in poor circumstances, and contrived to get some humble employment about the corporation property. It happened that about this time Tam Young – the last functionary who had a formal appointment and a regular salary, and who wore the executioner's official costume – was getting rather shaky, and accordingly Murdoch was retained as a sort of assistant or stand-by. On Young's death he got a monopoly of the trade, such as it is; but, as he had neither the official appointment nor the regular pay, he was remunerated by the job. He took to the work quite genially, and as he regarded his own functions as perfectly necessary to the good government, he did not fail to be on perfectly comfortable terms with himself. As his person became known in Glasgow, however, he found it convenient for his comfort to remove from the city, and took up his residence sometimes in Paisley, sometimes in Kilmarnock, sometimes in the adjacent villages – such as Motherwell, – and he has even been recognized officiating as a pastrybaker's assistant at one of our fashionable Clyde watering-places.

William Wallace, Words at his Trial

Sir Peter Mallorie, the king's justice, then rose, and read the indictment, wherein the prisoner was impeached as a traitor to his sovereign, the king of England; as having burnt the villages and abbeys, stormed the castles, and slain the liege subjects, of his master. 'To Edward,' said Wallace, 'I cannot be a traitor, for I owe him no allegiance; he is not my sovereign; he never received my homage; and whilst life is in this persecuted body, he never shall receive it. To the other points whereof I am accused, I freely confess them all. As governor of my country, I have been an enemy to all its enemies. I have slain the English; I have mortally opposed the English king; I have stormed and taken the towns, and castles, which he unjustly claimed as his own. If I, or my soldiers, have plundered or done injury to the houses, or to the ministers of religion, I repent me of my sin – but it is not of Edward of England that I shall ask pardon.'

William Wallace, 1270–1305

Flores Historiarum

About the feast of the assumption of the blessed Mary, a certain Scot, by name Wilhelmus Waleis, a man void of pity, a robber given to sacrilege, arson and homicide, more hardened in cruelty than Herod, more raging in madness than Nero, after committing aimless atrocities had assembled an army and opposed the King at Falkirk. This man of Belial, after numberless crimes, was seized by the King's agents, carried to London, condemned to a most cruel but justly deserved death, and suffered this, all in the manner prescribed by the sentence but with additional aggravations and indignities. He was drawn through the streets of London, at the tails of horses, until he reached a gallows of unusual height, specially prepared for him; there he was suspended by a halter, but afterwards let down half-living; next his genitals were cut off and his bowels torn out and burnt in a fire; then, and not till then, his head was cut off and his trunk cut into four pieces ... Behold the end of the merciless man, who himself perishes without mercy.

Matthew of Westminster, fl 1300

William Wallace on his way to execution. NMS

Memoirs of the Marquis of Montrose

On the morning of Tuesday the 21st of May 1650, Montrose was 'delicately' adjusting his head for the public exhibition of it which was to last for ten years. Those flowing auburn locks, cherished as the type of his loyalty, now dishevelled, and probably matted with the blood of his wounds, he was in the act of combing out and arranging, when a sullen moody man broke in upon him with the impertinent reproof, 'Why is James Graham so careful of his locks?' 'My head,' replied the hero, 'is yet my own; I will arrange it to my taste; tonight, when it will be yours, treat it as you please.'

Mark Napier, 1798–1879

The last scene in the life of Montrose, 1650, W T Davey after E M Ward.
City of Edinburgh Art Centre

On the eve of his execution

Let them bestow on every airt a limb,
Then open all my veins, that I may swim
To Thee, my Maker, in that crimson lake, –
Then place my par-boil'd head upon a stake,
Scatter my ashes – strew them in the air, –
Lord! since Thou knowest where all these atoms are,
I'm hopeful thou'lt recover once my dust,
And confident thou'lt raise me with the just.

James Graham, Marquis of Montrose, 1612–50

Kirkcaldy session records, 1633: the execution of William Coke and Alison Dick for witchcraft

Imprimis. To Mr. James Miller when he went to Prestowne for a man to try them, 47s.	£2	7	0
Item. To the man of Culross the executioner when he went away the first time, 12s.	0	12	0
Item. For coals for the witches, 24s.	1	4	0
Item. In purchasing the commission	9	3	0
Item. For one to go to Finmouth for the laird to sit upon their assize as judge	0	6	0
Item. For harden to be jumps to them	3	10	0
Item. For making of them	0	8	0
Summe for the Kirk's part Scots	17	10	0

The Town's part of Expences Debursed extraordinarily upon William Coke and Alison Dick:

Imprimis. For ten loads of coal to burn them, 5 merks	£3	6	8
Item. For a tar barrel, 14s.	0	14	0
Item. For towes	0	6	0
Item. To him that brought the executioner	2	18	0
Item. To the executioner for his pains	8	14	0
Item. For his expences here	0	16	4
Item. For one to go to Finmouth for the laird	0	6	0

Satan's Invisible World Discovered

About thirty years ago, more or less, there was one William Barton apprehended for Witch-craft. His confession was first, that if he had twenty Sons, he would advise them to shun the lust of uncleanness. For said he, I never saw a beautiful Woman, Maid, Nor Wife, but I did covet them, which was the only cause that brought me to be the Devils Vassal. ...

After this Confession he begged Liberty to sleep a little, which the Judges granted to him. After he had sleept a short time, he awakened with a great Laughter. The Judges inquired the reason. He replyed, being seriously urged, that the Devil had come to him, and rebuked him with angcr, and threatned him most furiously, that he had confessed, and bad him deny all, for he should be his Warrand.

After this, he turned obdured, and would never to his dying hour acknowledge any thing, for the Devil had perswaded him, even from his first ingaging, that no man should take his life, Which promise he firmly believed, to the very last. When they told him in the prison-house, that the Fire was built, and the Stake set up, and the executioner coming to bring him forth he answered he cared not for all that, for said he I shal not die this day. But the Executioner got presently orders to lead him forth, and he steping in at the Prison door in an instant shot to dead, as they say, and never stired again. In this strait, they appointed the Executioners Wife to strangle him, which she did willingly, a reward being promised to her. When the Warlock heard this, that a Woman was to put him to death, O, crys he, how hath the Devil deceived me? Let none ever trust to his Promises. All this was done at Kirkliston before famous witnesses. The Executioners name was Andrew Martain and his wifes name Margaret Hamilton, who when her Husband died clapt her hands, and cryed often, Dool for this parting, my dear burd Andrew Martin.

George Sinclair, d 1696

The Execution of Mary, Queen of Scots

Then with a smileing countenannce she turned herself to her men servannts Melvyn and the rest standing upon a benche neare unto the scaffold, who were sometimes weeping and sometimes crying out aloud, and continuallie crossing themselves and praied in lattin. And the said Queene (thus turned unto them) did herself likewise crosse them and bid them farewell & praied them to praie for her even to the last houre.

Scottish jewellery associated with Mary, Queen of Scots. The locket, from the Penicuik Jewels, is said to have been given by Mary to her servant Giles Mowbray just before her death. NMS

This done one of her women having a Corpus Christi clothe lapped it up three corner wise and kissed it and put it over the face of her Queene and Mistris and pinned fast on the call of her heade.

Then the two women mournefully departed from her and then the saide Queene, kneeled downe upon the cushion at which time verie resolutely without anie token of the fear of deathe, she spake aloude this psalme in lattin In the Domine confido ne confunder in aeternum & Then gropeing for the blocke she laied downe her head, putting her chaine over her back with both her handes, which holdeing there still, had byn cut of had they not byn espied. Then she laied herself upon the blocke most quietlie and stretching out her Armes and leggs cried out In manus tuas Domine & three or foure times. At last while one of the Execucioners held her straightlie with one of his handes, the other gave two strokes with an Axe before he did cut of her head and yet left a little gristle behind. At which time she made verie smale noise and stirred not anie part of herself from the place where she laid.

Then the executioner which cut of her head lifted it up and bad God save the Queene then her dressing of lawne fell from her head which appeared as Grey as if she had by three score and ten yeares old poled very short, her face being in a moment so much altered from the forme which she had when she was alive, as a fewe could remember her by her dead face, her lipps stirred up and downe for almost a quarter of an houre after her head was cutt of.

Then said Mr Deane so perish all the Queenes enemies. And afterwardes the Earle of Kent came to the dead bodie and standing over it, with a loud voice likewise said, such end happen to all the Queenes and the Gospells enemies.

Then one of the executioners pulling of her garters espied her little dogge which was under her clothes which could not be gotten forth but by force and afterwardes would not depart from her dead corpes but came and laid betweene her head and shoulders (a thing diligentlie noted) the same dogge being imbrued with her bloud was carried awaie and washed, as all things else were that had anie bloud, unles thos things which were burned. The executioners were sent awaie with monie for their fees not having anie one thing that belonged unto her. Afterwardes everie one was comannded forth of the hall saveing the Sheriff and his men who carried her up into a great chamber made readie for the Surgeons to embalme her, and there she was embalmed.

Robert Wyngfield, fl 1587

Memorial to the Wigtown Martyrs
Margaret Wilson and Margaret MacLachlan

Murter'd for ouning Christ Supreame
Head of his church and no more crime
But not abjuring presbytry,
And her not ouning prelacy.
They her condemned, by unjust law,
Of Heaven nor Hell they stood no aw.
Within the sea ty'd to a stake
She suffered for Christ Jesus sake.
The actors of this cruel crime
Was Lagg, Strachan, Winram and Grahame
Neither young yeares nor old age
Could stop the fury of their rage.

The drowning of the Covenanters Margaret MacLauchlan and Margaret Wilson. NMS

Covenanter's Deathbed

I canna dee, tho' I fain wud dee,
For I'm tired o' the world wide,
An' nae grave will ever be rest to me
But a grave on the green hill-side.

Bury me deep on the Bennan hill,
Whaur I may face the sea,
An' sleep a lang an' blessèd sleep
Till Christ shall wauken me.

Oh! to be quat o' life's stoury faucht
An' this dull hot bed o' pain,
Tae lie a' nicht in the windy waucht
O' the clear caul' mornin' rain:–

And the whaup may skirl in the lanely sky,
An' the sun shines miles aroon';
And quately the stately ships gae by,
But I'll be sleepin' soun'.

George Douglas Brown, 1869–1902

*Piece of the shroud of 'Bluidy MacKenzie', the title earned by Lord Advocate
Sir George MacKenzie (1636–91) in the 1680s for his actions against the
Covenanters. He was also founder of the Advocates Library, now the
National Library of Scotland. NMS*

Covenanters' Memorial

At Hamilton lie the heads of John Parker, James Hamilton, and Christopher Strang, who suffered at Edinburgh 7th December, 1666.

> Stay passenger, take notice
> What thou reads
> At Edinboro be our bodies
> Here our heads;
> Our right hands stood at Lanark
> These we want
> Because with them we sware
> The Covenant.

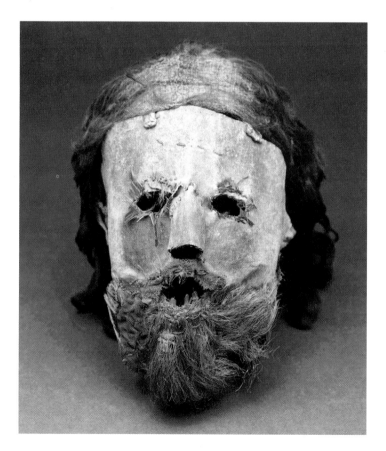

Mask of the Rev Alexander Peden, worn from about 1660 to 1670 to avoid recognition as he travelled around Scotland preaching at the banned open air services held by the Covenanters. NMS

When the devotions were over, the great bell began to toll, at half minute pauses, which had an awful and solemn effect. The criminals put on white caps, and Smith, whose behaviour was highly penitent and resigned, slowly ascended the platform. It is said Brodie tapped Smith on the shoulder, saying '*Go up, George, you are first in hand*'. He was raised a few feet above the scaffold, and placed immediately under the beam where the halters were fixed; he was followed by Brodie, who mounted with alertness and examined the dreadful apparatus with attention, particularly the halter designed for himself, which he pulled with his hand.

It was found that the halter had been too much shortened and they were obliged to be taken down to alter. During this dreadful interval, Smith remained on the platform trembling, but Brodie stepped briskly down to the scaffold, took off his night cap, and again entered into conversation with his friends, till the ropes were adjusted. He then sprung up again upon the platform but the rope was still improperly placed, and he once more descended, showing some little impatience, and observed that the executioner was a bungling fellow, and ought to be punished for his stupidity – but it did not much signify.

Having again ascended, he deliberately untied his cravat, buttoned up his waistcoat and coat, and helped the executioner to fix the rope; then pulling the night-cap over his face, he folded his arms, and placed himself in an attitude expressive of firmness and resolution. Smith, who, during the interruption, had been in fervent devotion, soon after the adjustment of the halters, let fall a handkerchief as a signal, and a few minutes before three the platform dropt, and they were launched into eternity. Thus ended the Life of William Brodie and of George Smith.

William Creech, 1745–1815

Kay's Portraits

In explanation of the wonderful degree of firmness, if not levity, displayed in the conduct of Brodie, a curious and somewhat ridiculous story became current. It was stated that he had been visited in prison by a French quack, of the name of Degravers, who undertook to restore him to life after he had hung the usual time; that, on the day previous to the execution, he had marked the temples and arms of Brodie with a pencil, in order the more readily to know where to apply the lancet; and that, with this view, the hangman had been bargained with a short fall. 'The excess of caution, however,' observes our worthy informant, who was himself a witness of

KAY DEL SULP

Mr BRODIE

*Deacon Brodie, respectable gentleman by day, burglar by night, designed the gallows
on which he himself was eventually hanged.* Kay's Portraits, NMS

he scene, 'exercised by the executioner, in the first instance, in shortening
the rope, proved fatal, by his inadvertency in making it latterly too long.
After he was cut down,' continues our friend, 'his body was immediately
given to two of his own workmen, who, by order of the guard, placed it in
a cart, and drove at a furious rate round the back of the Castle.' The object
of this order was probably an idea that the jolting motion of the cart might
be the means of resuscitation, as had once actually happened in the case

The execution of Deacon Brodie and George Smith, Alexander Ritchie.
City of Edinburgh Art Centre

of the celebrated 'half-hangit Maggie Dickson.'* The body was afterwards
conveyed to one of Brodie's own workshops in the Lawnmarket, where
Degravers was in attendance. He attempted bleeding, &c but all would not
do; Brad 'was fairly gone.'

* This woman had been executed for child-murder, and her body delivered
to her relatives for interment, who put it in a cart to transport it a few
miles out of town. Strange to say, half the journey was not accomplished,
when, to the consternation of those present, the poor woman revived.
She lived afterwards several years, and bore two children to her husband.

Hugh Paton, fl 1838

He had deserted in a blink of fine weather between the rains that splashed the glutted rat-runs of the front. He had done it quickly and easily, he told to Chae, he had just turned and walked back. And other soldiers that met him had thought him a messenger, or wounded, or maybe on leave, none had questioned him, he'd set out at ten o'clock in the morning and by afternoon, taking to the fields, was ten miles or more from the front. Then the military policemen came on him and took him, he was marched back and court-martialled and found to be guilty.

And Chae said to him, they sat together in the hut where he waited the coming of the morning, *But why did you do it, Ewan? You might well have known you'd never get free.* And Ewan looked at him and shook his head, *It was that wind that came with the sun, I minded Blawearie, I seemed to waken up smelling that smell. And I couldn't believe it was me that stood in the trench, it was just daft to be there. So I turned and got out of it.*

In a flash it had come on him, he had wakened up, he was daft and a fool to be there; and, like somebody minding things done in a coarse wild dream there had flashed on him memory of Chris at Blawearie and his last days there, mad and mad he had been, he had treated her as a devil might, he had tried to hurt her and maul her, trying in the nightmare to waken, to make her waken him up; and now in the blink of sun he saw her face as last he'd seen it while she quivered away from his taunts. He knew he had lost her, she'd never be his again, he'd known it in that moment he clambered back from the trenches; but he knew that he'd be a coward if he didn't try though all hope was past.

So out he had gone for that, remembering Chris, wanting to reach her, knowing as he tramped mile on mile that he never would. But he'd made her that promise that he'd never fail her, long syne he had made it that night when he'd held her so bonny and sweet and a quean in his arms, young and desirous and kind. So mile on mile on the laired French roads: she was lost to him, but that didn't help, he'd to try to win to her side again, to see her again, to tell her nothing he'd said was his saying, it was the foulness dripping from the dream that devoured him. And young Ewan came into his thoughts, he'd so much to tell her of him, so much he'd to say and do if only he might win to Blawearie ...

Then the military policemen had taken him and he'd listened to them and others in the days that followed, listening and not listening at all, wearied and quiet. *Oh, wearied and wakened at last, Chae, and I haven't cared, they can take me out fine and shoot me to-morrow, I'll be glad for the rest of it, Chris lost to me through my own coarse daftness. She didn't even come to give me a kiss at good-bye, Chae, we never said good-bye; but I mind the bonny head of her down-bent there in the close. She'll never know, my dear quean, and that's best – they tell lies about folk they shoot and she'll think I just died like the rest; you're not to tell her.*

And neither could remember that, it had vexed Ewan a while, and then he forgot it, sitting quiet in that hut on the edge of morning. Then at last he'd stood up and gone to the window and said *There's bare a quarter of an hour now, Chae, you'll need to be getting back.*

And they'd shaken hands, the sentry opened the door for Chae, and he tried to say all he could for comfort, the foreshadowing of the morning in Ewan's young eyes was strange and terrible, he couldn't take out his hand from that grip. And all that Ewan said was *Oh man, mind me when next you hear the peewits over Blawearie – look at my lass for me when you see her again, close and close, for that kiss that I'll never give her.* So he'd turned back into the hut, he wasn't feared or crying, he went quiet and calm; and Chae went down through the hut lines grouped about that place, a farm-place it had been, he'd got to the lorry that waited him, he was cursing and weeping then and the driver thought him daft, he hadn't known himself how he'd been. So they'd driven off, the wet morning had come crawling across the laired fields, and Chae had never seen Ewan again, they killed him that morning.

Lewis Grassic Gibbon, 1901–35

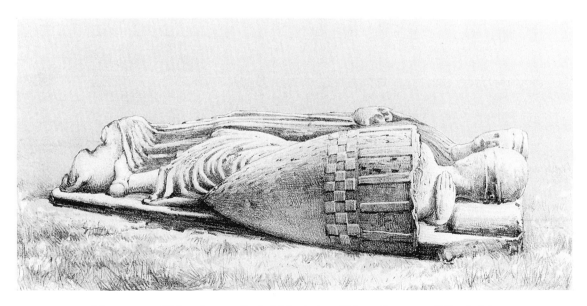

Monument to Walter Stewart, Earl of Mentieth and Mary, Countess of Mentieth in the Priory of Inchmahome. NMS

The Ballad of Grey Weather from *The Herd of Standlan*

When the wind is nigh and the moon is high
And the mist on the riverside,
Let such a fare have a very good care
Of the Folk who come to ride.
For they may meet with the riders fleet
Who fare from the place of dread;
And hard it is for a mortal man
To sort at ease with the Dead.

John Buchan, 1875–1940

The Death of Dear-meal Johnny

Oft his wraith had been seen gliding
'Mang the meal sacks i' the spence,
Till the house, folks scarce could bide in,
Terrified maist out o' sense.

'Neath his head the death-watch tinkled,
Constant as the lapse of time;
Frae his bed the dead licht twinkled,
Wi' its blue and sulphurous flame.

'Neath the bed auld Bawty scrapit,
A' day, thrang as thrang could be;
Made a hole, sae grave-like shapit,
Folk glowered quaking in to see.

On the dreary kirkyaird road, aye
By night he raised sic eldritch howls;
Weel he kenned his maister's body
Soon must mix amang the mools.

Frae the wattles dead-draps spatter'd;
At the can'les dead-speals hang;
Pyets rave the thack, and chatter'd;
In folk's lugs the dead-bell rang.

William Johnston, 'The Bard of Corrie', fl 1850

Wigtown and Whithorn: historical and descriptive sketches

Tradition has it that an enterprising packman lived in or near Wigtown long ago. He had a consignment of cloth on board a vessel which put into a local port. The ship was plague-stricken, and the people in the district, fearing that the infection might spread by means of the packman and his cloth, seized both the merchant and his wares, and taking them to Kirkwaugh dug a deep grave, in which they deposited – the packman alive. Even until lately people imagined they saw lights and heard knocks at the spot, which gets the name of the Packman's Grave to this day.

Gordon Fraser fl 1877

Antiquities of Scotland

Spedlins Tower is chiefly famous for being haunted by a bogle or ghost ... In the time of the late Sir John Jardine's grandfather, a person named Porteous, living in the parish of Applegarth, was taken up on suspicion of setting fire to a mill, and confined in the lord's prison, the pit or dungeon, at this castle. The lord being suddenly called to Edinburgh on some pressing and unexpected business, in his hurry forgot to leave the key of the pit, which he always held in his own custody. Before he discovered his mistake and could send back the key – which he did the moment he found it out – the man was starved to death, having first, through the extremity of hunger, gnawed off one of his hands. Ever after that time the castle was terribly haunted till a Chaplain of the family exorcised and confined the bogle to the pit, whence it could never come out, so long as a large Bible, which he had used on that business, remained in the castle. It is said that the Chaplain did not long survive this operation. The ghost, however, kept quietly within the bounds of his prison till a long time after, when the Bible, which was used by the whole family, required a new binding, for which purpose it was sent to Edinburgh. The ghost, taking advantage of its absence, was extremely boisterous in the pit, seeming as if it would break through the iron door, and making a noise like that of a large bird fluttering its wings. The Bible being returned, and the pit filled up, everything has since remained perfectly quiet.

Francis Grose, 1731–91

Old chapel in the burying-ground of the Macleods of Raasay.
Alasdair Alpin MacGregor

Letters on Demonology and Witchcraft

Upon the 10th of June, 1754, Duncan Terig, *alias* Clark, and Alexander Bain Macdonald, two Highlanders, were tried before the Court of Justiciary, Edinburgh, for the murder of Arthur Davis, sergeant in Guise's regiment, on the 28th September, 1749. The accident happened not long after the civil war, the embers of which were still reeking, so there existed too many reasons on account of which an English soldier, straggling far from assistance, might be privately cut off by the inhabitants of these wilds. It appears that Sergeant Davis was missing for years, without any certainty as to his fate.

At length, an account of the murder appeared from the evidence of one Alexander MacPherson (a Highlander, speaking no language but Gaelic, and sworn by an interpreter), who gave the following extraordinary account of his cause of knowledge: – He was, he said, in bed in his cottage, when an apparition came to his bedside and commanded him to

109

rise and follow him out of doors. Believing his visitor to be one Farquharson, a neighbour and friend, the witness did as he was bid; and when they were without the cottage, the appearance told the witness he was the ghost of Sergeant Davis, and requested him to go and bury his mortal remains, which lay concealed in a place he pointed out in a moorland tract called the Hill of Christie. He desired him to take Farquharson with him.

Next day the witness went to the place specified, and there found the bones of a human body much decayed. The witness did not at that time bury the bones so found, in consequence of which negligence the sergeant's ghost again appeared to him, upbraiding him with his breach of promise. On this occasion the witness asked the ghost who were the murderers, and received an answer that he had been slain by the prisoners at the bar. The witness, after this second visitation, called on the assistance of Farquharson, and buried the body.

Farquharson was brought in evidence to prove that the preceding witness, MacPherson, had called him to the burial of the bones, and told him the same story which he repeated in court. Isabel MacHardie, a person who slept in one of the beds which run along the wall in an ordinary Highland hut, declared that upon the night when MacPherson said he saw the ghost, she saw a naked man enter the house and go towards MacPherson's bed.

Sir Walter Scott, 1771–1832

Thrawn Janet

Mr Soulis was feared for neither man nor deevil. He got his tinder-box, an' lit a can'le, an' made three steps o't ower to Janet's door. It was a big room, as big as the minister's ain, an' plenished wi' grand, auld, solid gear, for he had naething else. There was a fower-posted bed wi' auld tapestry; and a braw cabinet of aik, that was fu' of' the minister's divinity books, an' put there to be out o' the gate; an' a wheen duds o' Janet's lying here and there about the floor. But nae Janet could Mr Soulis see; not ony sign of a contention. In he gaed (an' there's few that wad hae followed him) an' lookit a' round, an' listened. But there was naethin' to be heard, neither inside the manse nor in a' Ba'weary parish, an' naethin' to be seen but the muckle shadows turnin' round the can'le. An' then a' at aince, the minister's heart played dunt an' stood stock-still; an' a cauld wund blew amang the hairs o' his heid. Whaten a weary sicht was that for the puir man's een! For there was Janet hangin' frae a nail beside the auld aik cabinet: her heid aye lay on her shoother, her een were steeked, the tongue projekit frae her mouth, and her heels were twa feet clear abune the floor.

'God forgive us all!' thocht Mr Soulis; 'poor Janet's dead.'

He cam' a step nearer to the corp; an' then his heart fair whammled in his inside. For by what cantrip it wad ill-beseem a man to judge, she was hingin' frae a single nail an' by a single wursted thread for darnin' hose.

It's an awfu' thing to be your lane at nicht wi' siccan prodigies o' darkness; but Mr Soulis was strong in the Lord. He turned an' gaed his ways oot o' that room, and lockit the door ahint him; and step by step, doon the stairs as heavy as leed; and set doon the can'le on the table at the stairfoot. He coulnae pray, he couldnae think, he was dreepin' wi' caul' swat, an' naething could he hear but the dunt-dunt-duntin' o' his ain heart. He micht maybe have stood there an hour, or maybe twa, he minded sae little; when a' o' a sudden, he heard a laigh, uncanny steer upstairs; a foot gaed to an' fro in the cha'mer whaur the corp was hingin'; syne the door was opened, though he minded weel that he had lockit it; an' syne there was a step upon the landin', an' it seemed to him as if the corp was lookin' ower the rail and doon upon him whaur he stood.

He took up the can'le again (for he couldnae want the licht), and as saftly as ever he could, gaed straucht out o' the manse an' to the far end o' the causeway. It was aye pit-mirk; the flame o' the can'le, when he set it on the grund, brunt steedy and clear as in a room; naething moved, but the Dule water seepin' and sabbin' doon the glen, an' yon unhaly footstep that cam' ploddin' doun the stairs inside the manse. He kenned the foot ower weel, for it was Janet's; and at ilka step that cam' a wee thing nearer, the cauld got deeper in his vitals. He commended his soul to Him that made an' keepit him; 'and, O Lord,' said he, 'give me strength this night to war against the powers of evil.'

By this time the foot was comin' through the passage for the door; he culd hear a hand skirt alang the wa', as if the fearsome thing was feelin' for its way. The saughs tossed an' maned thegether, a lang sigh cam' ower the hills, the flame o' the can'le was blawn aboot; an' there stood the corp of Thrawn Janet, wi' her grogram goun an' her black mutch, wi' the heid aye upon the shoother, an' the girn still upon the face o't – leevin', ye wad hae said – deid, as Mr Soulis weel kenned – upon the threshold o' the manse.

It's a strange thing that the saul of man should be that thirled into his perishable body; but the minister saw that, an' his heart didnae break.

She didnae stand there lang; she began to move again an' cam' slowly towards Mr Soulis whaur he stood under the saughs. A' the life o' his body, a' the strength o' his speerit, were gowerin' frae his een. It seemed she was gaun to speak, but wanted words, an' made a sign wi' the left hand.

There cam' a clap o' wund, like a cat's fuff; oot gaed the can'le, the saughs skrieghed like folk; an' Mr Soulis kenned that, live or die, this was the end o't.

'Witch, beldame, devil!' he cried, 'I charge you, by the power of God, begone – if you be dead, to the grave – if you be damned, to hell.'

An' at that moment the Lord's ain hand out o' the Heevens struck the Horror whaur it stood; the auld, deid, desecrated corp o' the witch-wife, sae lang keepit frae the grave and hirsled round by deils, lowed up like a brunstane spunk and fell in ashes to the grund; the thunder followed, peal on dirling peal, the rairing rain upon the back o' that; and Mr Soulis lowped through the garden hedge, and ran, wi' skelloch upon skelloch for the clachan.

That same mornin' John Christie saw the Black Man pass the Muckle Cairn as it was chappin' six; before eicht, he gaed by the change-house at Kockdow; an' no lang after, Sandy M'Lellan saw him gaun linkin' doun the braes frae Kilmackerlie. There is little doubt but it was him that dwalled sae lang in Janet's body; but he was awa' at last; and sinsyne the deil has never fashed us in Ba'weary.

Robert Louis Stevenson, 1850–94

Witchcraft and Superstitious Record in the South-western District of Scotland

Many years ago a drover, while making his way north and crossing that wild and thinly populated district which lies between the head of the parish of Parton and the Moor of Corsock had the following uncanny experience: He had left the Parton district late in the afternoon with the intention of reaching a farm-house some miles north of the village of Corsock. By the time he reached the path over Corsock Hill, however, it had become dark, and occasional flashes of lightning foretold that a storm was at hand. With loud peals of thunder, vivid flashes of lightning, and a downpour of rain the storm at last broke. The only shelter near at hand was some thorn bushes by the roadside, under which the drover crept and stayed for fully an hour, while the storm raged and the darkness increased. When the storm had somewhat abated the drover set out once more, hurrying as fast as the darkness would allow him. He had reached a very desolate part of the moor when his collie gave a low whine and crept close to his master's heels. The drover stood up for a moment to try and find a reason for the dog's behaviour, when down in the glen between the hills he heard what at first appeared the sound of bagpipes, which increased

The headless piper. John Copland

quickly to a shrill piercing wailing that struck terror to his heart, the collie creeping closer and closer to his heel whining in a way that showed he was as much frightened as his master.

Standing irresolute, a blaze of blue light flashed right in front of him, in the centre of which appeared the figure of a piper, his pipes standing like horns against the background of blue light. The figure moved backwards and forwards playing the wildest of music all the time. It next seemed to come nearer and nearer, and the drover, now transfixed to earth with terror, saw that the piper was headless, and his body so thin that surrounding hills and country could be seen right through it. A blinding flash of fire, followed by an ear-splitting clap of thunder, brought matters to a close for the time being, and the drover fell prostrated among the heather. When he recovered his senses the strange light had gone, and with it the headless piper. The storm had cleared off, and in due time he reached the farm, where he was put up for the night. When he told his story no one spoke for a moment or two, then the farmer's aged father broke silence: 'Aye, aye, lad, ye hae seen the ghost o' the piper wha was murdered on his wey frae Patiesthorn. I hae had the same fearsome experience myself, tho' its mair than saxty years syne.'

J Maxwell Wood, 1868–1925, quoting a letter from John Copland

113

The wife of a Banffshire proprietor, of the minor class, had been about six months dead, when one of her husband's ploughmen, returning on horse-back from the smithy in the twilight of an autumn evening, was accosted, on the banks of a small stream, by a stranger lady, tall and slim, and wholly attired in green, with her face wrapped up in the hood of her mantle, who requested to be taken up behind him on the horse, and carried across. There was something in the tones of her voice that seemed to thrill through his very bones, and to insinuate itself in the form of a chill fluid between his skull and the scalp. The request, too, seemed a strange one; for the rivulet was small and low, and could present no serious bar to the progress of the most timid traveller. But the man, unwilling ungallantly to disoblige a lady, turned his horse to the bank, and she sprang up lightly behind him. She was, however, a personage that could be better seen than felt; and came in contact with the ploughman's back, he said, as if she had been an ill-filled sack of wool. And when, on reaching the opposite side of the streamlet, she leaped down as lightly as she had mounted, and he turned fearfully round to catch a second glimpse of her, it was in the conviction that she was a creature considerably less earthly in her texture than himself. She opened, with two pale, thin arms, the enveloping hood, exhibiting a face equally pale and thin, which seemed marked, however, by the roguish, half-humorous expression of one who had just succeeded in playing off a good joke. 'My dead mistress!' exclaimed the ploughman. 'Yes, John, *your mistress,*' replied the ghost. 'But ride home, my bonny man, for it's growing late; you and I will be better acquainted ere long.'

Hugh Miller, 1802–56

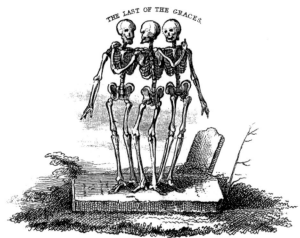

Ey! there wus a kin' o' ghaist or spectre use't take be seen at Dalarran, yt they ca't the Black Horseman, an folk said it wus the king o' the Danes yt wus kill't and bury't aneath the muckle leck, an couldna rest acause he wusna bury't at the Fintilach, at the ither side o' the water.

There wus yin George M'Millan, a son o' Brocklach's in Carsephairn, yt saw't, an tell't the doctor a' aboot it. It's no sae mony years sin he wus leevin in Manchester. It wus in 1809, and he wus takin his sister tae Dumfries tae the Boardin-skule, an she wus sittin ahint him on the beast; for it wus the fashion than for the women tae ride on the horse ahint the man, on a pillion. It wus the grey o' the mornin, for the Black Horseman wus never seen at nicht like ither ghaists, but ey whun it wus nearly daylicht. There wus nae brig ower the Garpel than, but just a ford, an whun they wur crossin't they heard the fit o' a beast comin doon the burn, an jaupin the water aboot wi its feet. They never thocht o' the Black Horseman, but wunner't wha could be comin doon the burn at that time i'e mornin, an sae they stoppit till it cam up.

They had har'ly stoppit whun it cam bye them, no half a dizzen yairds aff, an keepit strecht on doon the burn, sae yt they had a gude sicht o' him. The horse wus a big black yin, the biggest they had ever seen, an had an awfu queer saddle on, an something like airmour on its neck, but there wus naething fleysome aboot it; an the man wus a perfet giant, wi gude features an black hair, an he wus dress't in black airmour, an had on a helmet wi feathers on't, an he cairry't a big sword. He took nae notice o' them, an never loot on they wur there, an whun he had gane doon the burn a bit, he turn't on tae the haugh, an strecht for Dalarran stane. He stoppit there a minute, an then gaed richt across the holm, an through the Ken, an up the hillside.

Geordie wus curious tae ken whaur he gaed tae, an follow't him, but his horse walkit that fast they could har'ly keep up wi't. He gaed richt up the hill till he wun tae the muckle leck yt use't tae stan ablow the Fintilach hoose, an he stoppit there an gradually fadit awa oot o' their sicht.

Mony a yin had seen him at the ford, but naebuddy ever follow't him afore, an they a' gied the same description o' him, an thocht he had a verra melancholy coontenance. A haena heard o' him bein seen sin his grave wus hokit up. Folk said he wus the king o' the Danes yt wus kill't by Grier o' Lag at the time o' the Persecution.

Robert de Bruce Trotter, 1833–1907

Witchcraft and Superstitions Record in the South-western District of Scotland

Early last century, when the mail packet crossed from Portpatrick to Ireland, a carrier, who lived at High Ardwell, regularly journeyed backwards and forwards to Portpatrick to bring supplies for the district. On his way home he was more than once alarmed and troubled by a woman in white, who stopped his horse and even caused his cart to break down. Once, indeed, the horse was so affected that it became quite incapable of moving the load, compelling the carrier in great distress to unyoke, and, mounting the horse, to make for home. His fears were not much lessened by finding that the white lady was seated behind him.

The appearances of the ghost became more frequent as time went on, and eventually the white woman manifested a desire to embrace the carrier, indicating that if he yielded even only to listen once to her whispered devotion he might be freed altogether from future interference. The carrier, after a good deal of doubt and hesitation, at last yielded, but, wishing to have some substantial barrier between himself and his ghostly lover, stipulated that she should come to the little back-window of his cottage on a particular night. The appointed time came, but the carrier, still very doubtful had planned accordingly. Cautiously and partially was the window opened. The white figure was there. Bending down to what appeared to be the man's face – but what was really the skull of a horse held towards her – there was a swift savage thrust of the ghostly face and half of the protruding horse's skull was severed. Thwarted in this unexpected way, the evil spirit slunk away, muttering 'Hard, hard, are the banes and gristle of your face!'

J Maxwell Wood, 1868–1925

Witchcraft and Second Sight in the Highlands and Islands of Scotland

In the big church of Beauly (*eaglais mhor na manachain*, ie of the Monastery) mysterious and unearthly sights and sounds were seen and heard at night, and none who went to watch the churchyard or burial-places within the church ever came back alive. A courageous tailor made light of the matter and laid a wager that he would go any night, and sew a pair of hose in the haunted church. He went and began his task. The light of the full moon streamed in through the window, and at first all was silent and natural. At the dead hour of midnight, however, a big ghastly head

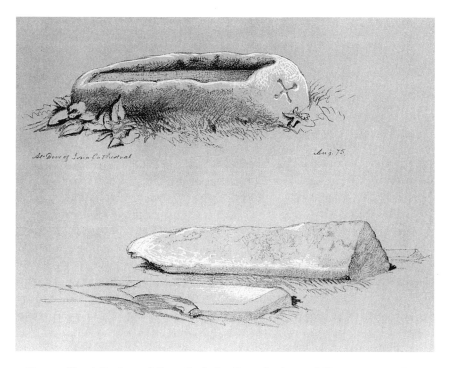

Stone coffin at the door of the cathedral at Iona. Sculptured Monuments in Iona
and the Highlands, by James Drummond, NMS

emerged from a tomb and said, 'Look at the old grey cow that is without food, tailor.' The tailor answered, 'I see that and I sew this,' and soon found that while he spoke the ghost was stationary, but when he drew breath it rose higher. The neck emerged and said, 'A long grizzled weasand that is without food, tailor.' The tailor went on with his work in fear, but answered, 'I see it, my son, I see it, my son; I see that and I sew this just now.' This he said drawling out his words to their utmost length. At last his voice failed and he inhaled a long breath. The ghost rose higher and said, 'A long grey arm that is without flesh or food, tailor.' The trembling tailor went on with his work and answered, 'I see it, my son, I see it, my son; I see that and I sew this just now.' Next breath the thigh came up and the ghastly apparition said, 'A long, crooked shank that is without meat, tailor.' 'I see it, my son, I see it, my son; I see that and I sew this just now.' The long foodless and fleshless arm was now stretched in the direction of the tailor. 'A long grey paw without blood, or flesh, or muscles, or meat, tailor.' 'I see it, my son, I see it, my son; I see that and I sew this just now,' while with a trembling heart he proceeded with his work. At last he had to draw breath, and the ghost, spreading out its long and bony fingers and clutching the air in front of him, said, 'A big grey claw that is without meat, tailor.' At that moment the last stitch was put in the hose, and the tailor gave one spring of horror to the door. The claw struck at him and the point of the fingers caught him by the bottom against the doorpost and took away the piece. The mark of the hand remains on the door to this day. The tailor's flesh shook and quivered with terror, and he could cut grass with his haunches as he flew home.

John G Campbell, 1836–91

Why we should believe in ghosts ...

A Lowlander once accepted some Skye people's dare to spend the night in a haunted house. All alone at midnight, he was disturbed by a beautiful young woman. 'Who are you?' he said. 'I am the ghost' she replied. But he did not believe her, and told her there were no such things as ghosts. 'That's a pity' said the lady 'for I have come to show you where the treasure is hidden. 'Oh well' said he 'that's a different story, where is it? 'And how can I tell you that? If there are no such things as ghosts, how can a ghost show you hidden treasure?'

And she vanished.

Traditional

Old rites, ceremonies, and customs of the inhabitants of the Southern counties of Scotland

Laird Harry Gilles of Littledean was extremely fond of hunting. One day as his dogs were pursuing a hare they suddenly stopped and gave up the pursuit. He being angry with his hounds, swore that the animal they had been in chase of must be one of the witches of Maxton. He had no sooner spoken, than the hares arose all around him so numerous, that they were springing over the saddle before him. His anger was so violent when he saw his hounds would not give them chase, that he jumped off his horse and killed them where they stood, all but one black one, who at that moment pursued a very large hare. He mounted his horse, and pursued the black greyhound, who had turned the hare and was coming directly towards him. It made a spring to clear his horse's neck, but the laird dexterously laid hold of one of her fore-legs, drew out his knife and cut it off; and very soon after the hares which were running so plentiful instantly disappeared. Next morning he heard that a woman of Maxton had lost her arm by an accident, which the informer could not account properly for. When the laird went to her house, he pulled the hare's foot, which had by this time changed into a woman's arm. He applied it, and found that she had been one of the hares, as it answered to the stump perfectly. She confessed the crime and was taken and drowned in the wiel, by the young men of the village that same day.

Thomas Wilkie, 1788–1838

Tam o' Shanter

By this time he was cross the ford,
Whare, in the snaw, the chapman smoor'd;
And past the birks and meikle stane,
Whare drunken Charlie brak's neck-bane;
And thro' the whins, and by the cairn,
Whare hunters fand the murder'd bairn;
And near the thorn, aboon the well,
Whare Mungo's mither hang'd hersel. –
Before him Doon pours a' his floods;
The doubling storm roars thro' the woods;
The lightnings flash from pole to pole;
Near and more near the thunders roll;
When, glimmering thro' the groaning trees,
Kirk-Alloway seem'd in a bleeze;
Thro' ilka bore the beams were glancing;
An' loud resounded mirth and dancing.
Inspiring bold John Barleycorn!
What dangers thou canst mak us scorn!
Wi' tipenny, we fear nae evil;
Wi' usquabae we'll face the devil! –
The swats sae ream'd in Tammie's noddle,
Fair play, he car'd na deils a boddle.
But Maggie stood right sair astonish'd,
Till, by the heel an' hand admonish'd,
She ventured forward on the light;

Coffins stood round, like open presses,
That shaw'd the dead in their last dresses;
And by some devilish cantraip slight
Each in its cauld hand held a light.

Illustration by John Faed for Tam O'Shanter by Robert Burns. NMS

An', wow! Tam saw an unco sight!
Warlocks and witches in a dance;
Nae cotillion brent new frae France,
But hornpipes, jigs, strathspeys, an' reels,
Put life an' mettle in their heels.
A winnock-bunker in the east,
There sat auld Nick, in shape o' beast;
A towzie tyke, black, grim an' large,
To gie them music was his charge:
He screw'd the pipes and gart them skirl,
Till roof and rafters a' did dirl. –
Coffins stood round, like open presses,
That shaw'd the dead in their last dresses;
And by some devilish cantraip sleight
Each in its cauld hand held a light. –
By· which heroic Tam was able
To note upon the haly table,
A murderer's banes in gibbet airns;
Twa span-lang, wee, unchristen'd bairns;
A thief, new-cutted frae a rape.
Wi' his last gasp his gab did gape;
Five tomahawks, wi' blude red-rusted;
Five scymitars, wi' murder crusted;
A garter, which a babe had strangled;
A knife, a father's throat had mangled,
Whom his ain son o' life bereft,
The grey hairs yet stack to the heft;
Wi' mair o' horrible an' awfu',
Which even to name wad be unlawfu'.

Robert Burns, 1759–96

Grizzel Grimme

Here lies with Death auld Grizzel Grimme,
Lincluden's ugly witch;
O Death, how horrid is thy taste
To lie with such a bitch!

Attributed to Robert Burns, 1759–96

Timor mortis conturbat me

I that in heill wes, and gladnes,
Am trublit now with gret seiknes,
And feblit with infermite.
Timor mortis conturbat me.

Our plesance heir is all vaneglory;
This fals warls is bot transitory;
The flesh is brukle the Fend is sle.
Timor mortis conturbat me.

The stait of man dois change and vary,
Now sound, now seik, now blith, now sary,
Now dansand mery, now like to dee.
Timor mortis conturbat me.

No stait in erd heir standis sickir:
As with the wind wavis the wickir,
Wavis this warldis vanite.
Timor mortis conturbat me.

On to the ded gois all estatis,
Princis, pelotis, and potestatis,

Baith riche and pur of all degre.
Timor mortis conturbat me.

He takis the knightis into feild,
Anarmit under helme and sheild:
Victour he is at all melle.
Timor mortis conturbat me.

That strang, unmerciful tyrand
Tak one the moderis breist sowkand
The bab, full of benignite.
Timor mortis conturbat me.

He takis the campion in the stour,
The capitane closit in the tour,
The lady in bour, full of bewte,
Timor mortis conturbat me.

He sparis no lord for his piscence,
Na clerk for his intelligence:
His awful strak may no man fle.
Timor mortis conturbat me.

Art magicianis and astrologgis,
Rethoris, logicianis and theologgis,
Thame helpis no conclusionis sle.
Timor mortis conturbat me.

In medicine the most practicianis,
Lechis, surrigianis and physicianis,
Thameself fra ded may not supple.
Timor mortis conturbat me.

I se that makaris amang the laif
Playis heir ther pageant, syne gois to graif:
Sparit is nought ther faculte.
Timor mortis conturbat me.

He has done petuously devour
The noble Chaucer, of makaris flour,
The Monk of Bery and Gower all thre.
Timor mortis conturbat me.

In Dunfermeline he has done roune
With Maister Robert Henrisoun;
Sir Johne the Ros enbrast has he.
Timor mortis conturbat me.

And he has now tane last of aw
Gud, gentil Stobo and Quityne Shaw,
Of wham all wichtis has pete.
Timor mortis conturbat me.

Gud Maister Walter Kennedy
In point of dede lyis veraly:
Gret reuth it wer that so suld be.
Timor mortis conturbat me.

Sen he has all my brether tane,
He will nought lat me lif alane:
On forse I man his nixt pray be.
Timor mortis conturbat me.

Sen for the ded remeid is none,
Best is that we for dede dispone,
Eftir our ded, that lif may we.
Timor mortis conturbat me.

William Dunbar, 1460–c1513

Epitaph, James Ramsay, Melrose 1751

The earth goeth on the earth
Glittering like gold
The earth goeth to the earth
Sooner than it would
The earth builds on the earth
Castles and Towers
The earth says to the earth
All shall be ours.

TUTTO FINISCE

Epitaph

Here lie I, Martin Elginbrodde:
Hae mercy o' my soul, Lord God,
As I wad do, were I Lord God,
And ye were Martin Elginbrodde.

Glossary

abune: above
ahint: behind
airns: irons
airt: quarter
ava: at all
ben: in
blitter: bittern
boddle: small coin
bore: hole
brand: sword
brukle: weak
brunstane spunk: burning match
brunt: burnt
buss: bush
but and ben: two-room cottage
bydeit: stayed
callant: youth
cantrip: trick
carle: man
caul, cauld: cold
chappin': striking
clachan: village
cracked: chatted
creepie: stool
croosely: cheerfully
dawding: gusting
den: narrow valley
dirlin': piercing
dispone: prepare
dool: sorrow
douce: pleasant
dowie: dismal
dreich: dreary
dunt: thump
erd: earth
ettlin': trying
fashed: bothered
faucht, fecht: fight
fit: foot
fleysome: terrifying
forfeuchen: breathless
fuff: hiss
gab: mouth

gar: cause to
ghaist: ghost
girn: grimace
goud: gold
gumpheon: funeral banner
haugh: river meadow
hause-bane: collarbone
heich: high
heill: health
hirsled: moved
hoggie: young sheep
hokit: dug
host: a bad cough
houms: river meadows
hurl: ride
ilka: every
jalouse: suppose
jaupin: splashing
laigh: low
leck: stone slab
linn: waterfall
litt: dye
loot on: let on
makaris: poets
maukin: hare
mercat: market
mools: mould, earth
muckle: great, big
mutch: cap
out o' the gate: out of the way
piscence: power
pit-mirk: pitch black
ples: please
poled: cut
pyets: magpies
quaich: drinking bowl
quean: young woman
rave: thieve
ream'd: frothed
reuth: pity
saugh: willow
scrievin': smoothly
scroggie: crooked

siccan: such
sicht: sight, view
sickir: certain
skelloch: yell
skirl: cry
smoor'd: smothered
snell: biting
souter: cobbler
sowkand: sucking
speir: ask
spence: store
steeked: protruding
steekit: shut
steer: movement
stoury: difficult
streak: lay out
sturt: trouble
swats: beer
sweir: reluctant
syne: ago
tap: public house
thack: thatch
theek: line
thirled: bound
thrang: busy
thrawn: perverse, twisted
tipenny: weak ale
tod: fox
towzie: rough
truffs: turf over a grave
usquabae: whisky
vogie: conceited
wame: belly
wat: know
weans: children
weasand: windpipe
wecht: weight
weel kent: well known
whammled: turned over
whilk: which
winnock-bunker: window seat
yin: one
yird: earth

Index